RETURN TO JOY

RETURN TO JOY

*A Family's Initiation into
the Mysteries of Dementia*

Charlotte Parker & Virginia Parker

Dancing Horse Publishing, LLC
Dallas, Texas

Dancing Horse Publishing, LLC
7111 Twin Tree Lane, Dallas, TX 75214
www.returntojoythebook.com

A goodmedia communications, llc book.
Book design by goodmedia communications, llc
Book cover design by Michael Albee of goodmedia communications, llc
Author photo by Mathew Butler of goodmedia communications, llc
The text in this book is set in Book Antiqua.
Manufactured in the United States of America.

Parker, Charlotte, 1944-
   Return to Joy: A Family's Initiation into the Mysteries of Dementia / Charlotte and Virginia Parker. --1st ed.
   p. cm.
   LCCN 2009925713
   ISBN-13: 9780982285107
   ISBN-10: 0982285108
      1. Parker, Kathryn, 1918- 2. Dementia--Patients--Biography. 3. Parker, Charlotte, 1944-
4. Parker, Virginia, 1948- 5. Mothers and daughters--Biography. 6. Caregivers--Biography. 7.
Dementia--Patients--Care. 8. Archetype (Psychology)   I. Parker, Virginia, 1948-
II. Title.

RC522.P37 2009   362.196'83'00922
                        QBI09-600048

To our precious baby Kathryn

Praise For Return to Joy ...

This is a beautiful book that will stir your heart and at the same time teach you how to be with someone who has dementia. It is full of feeling and yet not sentimental. It has excellent suggestions, but it is full of touching stories. Two sisters speak to us and to each other with an intimacy that is inspiring. This modest book could help thousands of people deal daily with their parents and loved ones, seeing challenges as opportunities for deep love and spiritual development.

- Thomas Moore, Author of *Care of the Soul*

Return to Joy reveals the fertile potential in what may seem a devastating process. It describes the healing and discoveries that unfolded among the family members, individually and in relationship, and it celebrates the many forms of community that arose around taking care of this woman. This will be an easy, heartening, and useful read for anyone whose life is touched (past, present or future) by Dementia's spreading reach.

- *Mount Shasta Magazine*

In *Return to Joy*, the Parker daughters realistically describe the descent of their Mother into the underworld where, having lost her memory, she lives now in the eternal Now. Their description is loving, informed, thoughtful, provocative, and of great value to all of us—whether we are presently dealing with the decline of a loved one or not. Their voyage touches all the islands of hope, despair, insight, frustration, and, finally, arrives home through a redemptive enlargement of loving consciousness.

- James Hollis, Ph.D., Jungian Analyst & Author
What Matters Most and *Why Good People Do Bad Things*

Practical, personal and compelling—*Return to Joy* is an invaluable guide to dealing with the challenges—physical, psychological, and spiritual—of dementia. This book is filled with practical information and creative strategies for negotiating the day-to-day challenges involved in caring for a loved one with this disorder. *Return to Joy* is an invaluable guide for those caring for a loved one with dementia.

-Nancy Dougherty, M.S.W., LCSW, Jungian Analyst, Co-Author of *The Matrix and the Meaning of Character*

This book is a must-read for any and all whose lives have been touched by the specter of dementia.

- Carolyn M. Bates, Ph.D., Jungian Analyst

Anyone who has cared for, or may one day care for, another will find this book a welcome compendium of the trials, tribulations, and blessings of this formidable mission as well as a guide into how to access its rich psycho-spiritual potential.

-Jacqueline West, Ph.D., Jungian Analyst, Co-Author of *The Matrix and the Meaning of Character*

This book moved me, challenged me to think, accurately instructed me, and offered many practical tips for dealing with the many everyday issues that arise in caring for adults with dementia. That's a lot to offer in one book, and the authors bring it off.

- Robert C. Atchley, Ph. D., Distinguished Professor of Gerontology (Emeritus), Miami University, Oxford, Ohio

Return to Joy is a jewel. This book shines light
on the collectively dreaded dementia occurring
in very many of our lives. The simple integrity
in writing of this shared process offers concrete
help, psychological depth as well as creative and/
or spiritual paths through seeming chaos. As a
psychotherapist for forty years and a Jungian
analyst I can say with deep respect that this
book offers an example of what individuation
discoveries are possible when we work with our
problems from inside out.

-Deanne Kreis Newman, LISW, Jungian Analyst

This tale of two sisters and how they came
together to face the world of dementia with
their mother is an inspirational one. This book
offers not only a practical guide for others
facing such painful circumstances, but delves
into deeper realms where love is entwined
with time-honored wisdom and ultimately the
human soul.

- Dick Russell, Author of *Black Genius* and
Eye of the Whale.

Return to Joy, is a profound, inspiring, and
touching book! A pleasure to read!

- Patricia Berry, Ph.D.

Our grateful and heartfelt thanks go to the following people. Kathy McDaniel and Irene McDaniel, our extended family. Thank you for your friendship and steadfast companionship over the past thirty-seven years. Sam Parker—Uncle Sam, thank you for your constant availability, musical contribution, and loving support. Your music heals our hearts and souls. Jimmie Kennedy, thank you for the many hours you spent with Kathryn. Your generosity is a saving grace. Carolyn Ankenman, your friendship with Kathryn enabled her to live independently for as long as she did. We are all eternally grateful to you. Elizabeth Fashola, your laughter and sweetness was a gift. Sandra Johnson, your larger than life, spirit-filled persona brought great joy to all our lives. Donna Collins, thank you for your friendship, support, hard work, and blessing of the ranch.

Dora Schenk, thank you for your friendship and willingness to be present with Kathryn along every step of her journey. Ron Schenk, your grounding energy, authoritative presence, and willingness to embrace the humor has deepened our love. Ashley Schenk—Kathryn's only grandchild, your spiritual communion with Kathryn has served as a guide. Thank you. Joan Anderson, your daily companionship, and precious friendship has been invaluable. We cannot imagine this experience without you at our side. Stella Rodriquez, Ph.D., you gave us hope. Thank you. Geraldine Warner, your friendship and nurturance was so needed and appreciated. Thank you. Susanne McClean, thank you in advance. Mary Louise Goyen—Kathryn's big sister, thank you for your love and support. Marguerite Nichols—Kathryn's lifelong friend, your memory lives long in our hearts.

It is not often that a simple story yields so much. My friends, Charlotte and Virginia Parker, tell the extraordinary story of their mother's dementia and how this disease transformed their lives. It would be a mistake to believe this story is only a documentation of a family journey into immeasurable loss and the sobering reality of old age and dementia — although on one level it is. This book is also a practical how-to and how-not-to. But for a reader who is willing to be guided by greater mysteries, this informative and inspiring book yields many treasures that touch and transform the heart. However, it is the mysteries that I would like to allude to because I witnessed the transformative power that reached across cultures, language, and time and brought forth a true sense and expression of joy.

This is an unusual volume that is filled with a treasure chest of jewels — the jewels of role-flipping, emotion-laden paradoxes, and the glittering solace of spiritual grace and comfort. These jewels were revealed through the initiations of choice and celebration. My friends gave their hearts to the mystery not the journey. They were pulled by the gravity and sorrow of Demeter and Persephone, that most ancient and compelling story of mother and daughter. They acquired a pomegranate consciousness. They learned how to choose their mother now and how to choose for their mother's dignity always. They gathered attendants rather than medical professionals that became a fellowship of friendship and nurturance where delight and compassion formed the cradle and community of care for their still loving, yet essentially different, charge.

Their lives were also graced by the evolving possibilities of the beckoning and open arms of Our Lady Guadalupe, the Mother of Americas — a spiritual mother forever present. They received the grace and consolation of celebration. The initiation into joy softened reality. It made everyone revisit and discover possibilities in relationships long hardened and made thorny and tarnished by time. There are other initiations that await readers. I leave those treasures to be discovered by new initiates into joy.

The enduring gift to be taken away from this book is the privilege of bearing witness to the most rare form of love beyond duty. This volume is a true expression of moral beauty.

- Stella Rodriquez, Ph.D.

Fairy tales, mysteries, religious doctrine, and parables are all derivatives of primal myths told in all cultures to answer questions about the psyche regarding human nature, human relations, connections with the Divine, and the origin of Man. Throughout the ages, fundamental psychological structures have emerged in the stories societies look to for answers regarding questions about creation, procreation, and spirituality, as well as everyday human behaviors. Contemporary cultures and individuals draw from these stories that have been passed on through pictorial images, storytelling, literature, film, and other art forms. In a larger sense, these stories write us; myths create us as they emerge from a realm that encompasses our consciousness. We find our connections to myth in different ways, just as myths connect with us in different ways.

Carl Jung coined the term, collective unconscious, as a way of explaining a common underlying psychic structure present in all people. Jung explained that consciousness is only part of a totality in which it is constantly interacting with contents and dynamics that are unconscious, not part of our everyday awareness. He thought of the contents of the unconscious as consisting in personal, and more fundamentally, in archetypal forms.

Archetypes are universal metaphors or tendencies expressing themselves in cultures and individuals throughout the ages in common images, patterns of behavior, and attitudes. Archetypes govern the entire range of human experience and express themselves culturally through such mythical modes as the stories and mysteries of ancient Greece and the legends and imagery surrounding the Catholic religious figure, Our Lady of Guadalupe. Archetypes work and play through individuals in everyday consciousness and behavior as well as in dream imagery and artistic endeavors.

Our immediate and extended family and friends sense the importance of ancient mysteries, mythologies, and the archetypal expressions of the soul in our lives and relationships. While we usually do not grasp the particular myth at hand, through our sensibility of the initiation we experienced through the journey with our mother and her dementia, we have come to consider life itself as ultimately a mystery in which we find ourselves alternately participating and witnessing, bringing out the best and worst of us with its joys and its sorrows, its ugliness and its beauty.

Chapter One

🌳

Demeter & Persephone

Be open to experiencing the humor that resides in the world of dementia.

Demeter and Persephone, or Kore as she is also known, are often referenced as the archetypal Mother and Daughter of Greek mythology. Their relationship with one another, as well as their individual dominions as goddesses, represent much of what is universally characteristic in being a mother or a daughter. Their story is an important framework for understanding a mother's love for her daughter and a daughter's mixed feelings toward her mother. Demeter and Persephone are the heroines of our mother's story. They are the primordial images that rose from the depths of our psyches to replay their roles in our lives.

Demeter is the goddess of the harvest, and her providence the cultivation of the soil. She is also known for her fierce attachment to her daughter, Persephone. Demeter, as are all of the Greek goddesses, is known for her daily involvement in the lives of mortals. While, like all the gods, she became engaged with mortals when it suited her own interests and came to the aid of "special" mortals she favored, Demeter, as goddess of fertility, was thought of as the nurturer of humankind. Demeter is also one of the goddesses who modeled the human experience of suffering and grief through loss, having felt it profoundly herself in relation to her daughter.

Demeter loved Persephone with the steadfastness only a mother knows. As Persephone became an adolescent, she grew to be beautiful and carefree. She danced playfully and picked wildflowers in the meadow near her home with her maiden friends. One afternoon as Persephone reached over to pick a narcissus flower, the earth opened, and Hades, god of the underworld, appeared and abducted her to be his bride in the subterranean depths. All of this occurred by arrangement with Zeus, king of the gods and father of Persephone.

Upon realizing her daughter was missing, Demeter embarked on a long journey in search of Persephone. On her journey she encountered many mortals and performed many miracles. On one occasion, she met a poor, elderly man who was gathering firewood. He invited her to return to his home to eat dinner with his family and to rest from her journey. When she told him that she was searching for her daughter, he wished her success and told her that he understood her suffering. The man's son was gravely ill and was not expected to live to see the sun rise. Demeter changed her mind and went with the kind man, stopping only once to gather some poppies by the path. Entering his humble home, Demeter went straight to the boy's bedside and kissed him on the cheek. Immediately the pallor left his face and his breathing eased. Demeter's gesture had restored the boy to full health. As one who was herself wounded, Demeter embraced the art of healing.

Demeter continued her search for her daughter and soon encountered Hecate, goddess of the crossroads. Hecate advised her to speak with Helios, the sun god, knowing Helios would have seen what happened to Persephone from his high place in the sky. Helios told Demeter what he had seen: Persephone had been kidnapped by Hades and taken to the underworld.

Feeling betrayed, Demeter renounced her divine duties including bringing fertility to the land. She left Mount Olympus swearing that the earth would remain barren until her daughter was returned to her. Demeter took refuge in the city of Eleusis and there, disguised as an old woman, she met the city ruler's two young daughters at the well. The girls took an immediate liking to her and asked Demeter home to meet their mother Metaneira. There she saw the mother, who was cuddling her infant son Demophoon. This stirred Demeter's longing for Persephone, and she once again became deeply depressed.

Everyone tried to cheer up the guest, but Demeter was inconsolable. Two members of the household decided to take matters into their own hands. Iambe, the lame daughter, tried to ply her to no avail with barley water and comically lascivious verses. Then Baubo, a middle-aged servant sat in front of Demeter and began talking, mostly making humorous and rather risqué comments. Encouraged when she saw

Demeter beginning to smile, Baubo hiked up her skirt and exposed herself to the goddess. Finally, Demeter responded with a deep belly laugh. Her good nature now restored, Demeter was employed to work as a nursemaid to the infant son.

Caring for him lovingly, feeding him on the nectar and ambrosia of the gods, Demeter grew attached to the young Demophoon and decided to make him immortal. Just as the goddess was holding him over the fire, the ritual that would transform him into an Olympian god, Metaneira entered the room. Mistakenly believing that Demeter was about to burn her son, she began to scream. Demeter angrily revealed herself as a goddess and berated the mother for interrupting the ritual that would have given her son immortality. She also demanded that a temple be built in her honor. Demeter remained in Eleusis, sitting alone in the darkness, once again depressed and grieving for her lost daughter.

All this time, the earth had grown barren and the harvests had ceased. The earth experienced a winter without end. Zeus finally realized what was happening and sent messengers pleading Demeter's forgiveness and coaxing her to return. Demeter refused to return until Persephone was given back to her. Meanwhile, as Persephone was held hostage in the underworld, Hades offered her a pomegranate to eat. Those who ate anything in the underworld were not allowed to return to the earth. Although Persephone had refused all food while she had been held captive, she accepted the pomegranate eating only the seeds, an act which sealed her fate to be Queen of the Underworld.

Zeus was now confronted with the claims of the two gods, Hades and Demeter, for possession of Persephone. He resolved the conflict through compromise, by allowing Persephone to return to the earth for nine months of the year. Demeter resumed her divine duties and restored the fertility of the earth during this time.

Thus, each year Demeter longs for her absent daughter and withdraws her favors from the earth for a period we know as winter, but Persephone returns each spring to end her desolation. Ultimately, Demeter withdrew to reside in her temple in Eleusis where she had enjoyed the welcome and support of mortals during her long search for Persephone. There she developed the Eleusian mysteries, a series of profoundly religious initiation ceremonies.

This story is an expression of a fundamental dynamic experienced between mothers and daughters in all times and places, each person alternately taking one of the roles of Demeter or Persephone in relation to the other.

In the story of our life experience with our mother, different aspects of the Demeter and Persephone myth present themselves as do others: separation, abandonment, loss, wandering, discovering, creating, lamenting, laughing, learning, wounding and healing, and above all, transforming.

Chapter Two

Daughter as Mother & Sister

Charlotte Parker

The loss of some memories is a blessing.

There are defining moments in life that shape the way we perceive society, and the way in which those in society perceive us. These moments mold our way of being so intensely that our true self — our authentic self — is pushed into the far corners of our being. Much like a fire that has been reduced to burning embers remains at a slow burn, my mother had a burning inside her that remained hot enough to maintain its life, but never hot enough to burn as brightly as I believe it once did. Old photographs of my mother portray a woman who was joyful, playful, and seemingly fulfilled. I never had the opportunity to see that woman as her daughter growing up. Photos of her smiling playfully seem to indicate a happy place that she knew but could not allow herself to live in as a woman.

My mother was a natural-born scientist. It was always my personal belief that she compromised her instinctual calling to the field of science in order to take on the obligatory roles of wife and mother. Mom suffered no confusion of her personal and professional interests. She was a woman of certainty and passion, and her interests were rooted in matters of the mind and the mysteries of the earth. She attended Rice University and the University of Texas and graduated with a degree in Geology. During her brief time as a career woman, after college and before marriage, she worked as a paleontologist for an oil company in Houston, Texas. She was thoroughly in her element in this role. Browsing through old photographs, one can see a gleam in her eyes at this time. As a scientist, both professionally and innately, she had an independence of mind that freed her from the normal constraints of societal convention and sentiment. She was as imaginative as she was constant and a perfectionist in many areas. If she were a young woman now, I believe she would have remained a professional scientist dedicated to academia rather than following the path of marriage and family.

Mom did not consider herself a victim of circumstance. She was born in 1918, and due to the social orientation of the times, it would never have occurred to her that marriage and children were not her destiny. When Mom was twenty-five, single, and verging on what was considered at the time "old-maid" status, she met my father.

Grandmother rode the streetcar back and forth to work teaching school. One day while riding home, she sat next to a woman who explained she had a handsome young U.S. Army Captain visiting who needed a date that evening. Grandmother mentioned her daughter and before the two parted ways at the next stop phone numbers had been exchanged. I am not sure if it was love at first sight, but there was a war going on and they did not date long before they became engaged. In a sense, one might consider all marriages are matters of Zeus, Hades, and Persephone.

My parents married in 1943. Within a year of marriage, my mother became pregnant and my father was sent overseas to fight in the war. This was a time of terrible loss and grief for my mother. I arrived at the same time that my maternal grandparents divorced and my mother's brother was killed in the line of duty. Suffering the loss of her son and husband, my grandmother opened her home to my mother and her sister (whose husband was also fighting overseas) along with both of their new babies. A form of Eleusis was being established in Houston.

My cousin and I began our lives in a grief-stricken home with a heartbroken grandmother, and mothers who had simultaneously lost their careers as well as their brother, and were living without the emotional support of their newlywed husbands or father. I now see my cousin and myself as being something like vessels containing the sadness of our mothers and grandmother. These women needed something in which to pour their grief, and we were it. From a mythological perspective, as an infant I was ironically already both Persephone lost to the underworld and Demeter grieving for my lost love object. Removed from my mother emotionally, I wandered through my childhood and adult life finding temporary ways to exist without the fundamental ground of a nurturing mother-daughter relationship.

I was eighteen-months-old when my father came home from the war. My parents purchased a home in the suburbs of Houston, bought a new car, and two years later, gave birth to a new baby girl. My father took a management position with the Coca-Cola Company, and life went on as it did for so many other American families. From the outside peering in, we were a picture-perfect unit, but intimacy was missing. When I was emotionally hungry, I would scrounge in the refrigerator; the "ice box" was the nurturer in our house. Our home life maintained just enough heat to sustain itself, but never enough to burn brightly.

Mom's personality was changed by marriage and family life. Though she certainly never said so, I believe marriage and motherhood were disappointments that prevented her from fully experiencing her own story. She did, however, provide some compensation for herself in keeping with the tradition of the women in our family, for whom the message was always clear — marriage is something to be endured by women as an alternative to being completely on your own, but one must always have a back-up plan. For most of the women in my family, Plan B was teaching. Like the others, Mom obtained a teaching certificate, and though my parents remained married, Mom used her training to take a position as a science teacher. She demonstrated an enthusiasm in her work that mothering did not give her, and I was again simultaneously Persephone held in the underworld and Demeter experiencing her loss.

Demeter was known to the Greeks for her beauty and her perfectionism; Mom always made her appearance impeccable. Her sense of style was perfectly defined, and I took pride in her beauty. I was envious of the doting affection my friends received from their mothers, but I could also take satisfaction in the admiration my mother evoked from my friends.

My childhood carried on. I maintained an emotional distance from my mother. I wanted her to notice me, and I think quite possibly, she did not want to be noticed by me. She disappeared in her schoolwork and her garden, and I wandered about.

My first day of Kindergarten is one of my most vivid childhood memories. I woke with the usual wave of both fear and excitement in regard to the unknown experience that was awaiting me that day. My mother ushered me to the school bus and sent me on my way to my first day of school, another form of a trip to the underworld. I arrived with no idea of what to do or where to go. I was alone and confused, dwelling terrified for several minutes in a sort of Hades. Thankfully a kind teacher rescued me as I stood in front of the school sobbing from loneliness and a feeling of abandonment. That afternoon I got back on the bus by myself. I had been forced to become a big girl through the day. At five years old, I understood I was on my own in this world.

As years went by, I continued wanting to have Mom waiting for me at the door like my friends' mothers. Instead, like Demeter, I had to go looking for her. I usually found her in the garden digging in the soil and tending to her plants. Mom always acted surprised, as though she had no idea I would come home. I found that so strange. I could not wait to get home to see her, and she seemed so taken aback and strangely resistant to seeing me.

At times, my desire to be noticed took me to extremes. I was so certain that Mom was oblivious to my existence that one day I decided to take matters into my own hands by hiding in a closet and attempting to force her to take note of my absence. From a mythological perspective, I was Persephone creating her own underworld in order to create a searching Demeter. My plan did not work. I sat bored and alone in the dark closet listening to the activities of my family. No one realized I was missing. I eventually retreated, bored and forlorn, to my room, myself the grieving Demeter in the halls of Eleusis.

Eventually, the sadness I felt in my relationship with my mother resolved itself into an underlying resentment—a resentment I used to veil an even deeper loneliness, hurt, and feeling of being unloved and perhaps unworthy of love. I was caught in an under-worldly trap, deeply resentful of my mother for not seeing me, and at the same time paradoxically making myself invisible through that very shroud of resentment.

Our family went through all the familial motions of mid-century Americans. Having never gained the attention I needed from my mother, I left home at the earliest opportunity. However, no matter how far away I went from Mom, I never stopped seeking out the woman who shined through in the photographs of her childhood. In my adulthood, I never blamed my mother for her disappointment in marriage and motherhood, but I did grieve the absence of the mother I desired in my life. Then after many years, one day I met her. Deep in the depths of a dementia that had taken her over, a little fire began to spark. Layer by layer the disappointments of my mother's life began to lift.

We all have secrets that will go with us to the grave, but, just as many with dementia forget their old familial hostilities, my mother no longer remembers her secrets. The blessing of Lethe, the mythical river of forgetfulness, is the paradoxical forgiving quality of dementia. With the loss of those secrets, Mom eventually emerged a happy woman. After she lost the capacity to be a mother, she gained a sincere and playful love that displaced the years of sorrow. In the depths of dementia, my mother returned to joy.

Virginia Parker

A person's "essence" remains even after dementia steals the personality. Continue to connect with that essence.

My debut into this world could not have been more different than my sister's. Whereas Charlotte's first four years were spent with grieving—perhaps even angry and certainly emotionally preoccupied—women suffering the death and loss of war, mine were spent in a happy relief brought on by our family's and America's return to normalcy. Happy — the lifelong name given to my father by a young Charlotte who could not quite pronounce "pappy" — was home from the war, Kathryn, our mother, was in her own new home having moved out of her mother's home, and I was the living, breathing evidence of a fresh start in life. As a family, we were whole and complete. Life was normal. Our family, and even the nation, was experiencing an era of abundance filled with a sense of security that our future was stable and safe. Blessed by fate's timing and full of energy, smiles, and mischief, I captured the attention denied to my sister.

As a hyperactive tomboy, I required attention and oversight. While I was never in serious trouble, my parents and schoolteachers always had one eye on me, which only served to intensify my desire for independence and autonomy.

While it is inarguable that all adults are certainly the emotional sums of their perceived childhood experiences, we often only bring focus to the "issues" that have left us flawed in some way. The parents of our childhood are often defined by the hurt, the loss, the grief, or the abandonment that we experienced as children. I do not remember my parents as individuals functioning in society; I simply remember them as Happy and Kathryn—guardians of my life. In his writings, Carl Jung emphasizes the reality of experience in the development of the emerging archetype in the psyche of a child. He eloquently explains in his book, *The Archetypes and the Collective Unconscious*, "The primitive mentality does not invent myths, it experiences them." While my perception of Kathryn was not directly one from the perspective of Demeter or Persephone, I can look at how Charlotte's separateness from Kathryn has mythically molded her personality and the choices she has made throughout her life. I recognize Demeter and Persephone at play in the relationship of Kathryn and Charlotte, and in retrospect, I can relate to the myth in my own connection with each of them.

Happy and I did not develop an adult relationship before his death. Although I have always had a great deal of respect for Kathryn, I have come to understand her as a mother more through Charlotte's perception and experience than through my own relationship with her. My pre-teen and teenage memories of Kathryn are clearer than my early childhood memories. Like Persephone, Charlotte was beautiful, popular, social and regularly taken away from me by the long arms of Hades in the form of heart-pounding boys. I do not remember a single Friday or Saturday evening that she spent at home. She had a date every weekend night of her high school life. By the time I was in high school, Charlotte was attending university, and my father was traveling frequently. Consequently, my pre-teen and teenage years included a good deal of time spent with Kathryn. Because she had never been one for maternal doting and affection, our relationship naturally parlayed into a friendship. We watched television, played chess, attended sports events, and shopped. Kathryn was an enthusiastic shopper, and I was an avid athlete. I accompanied her on many a trip to the mall, while she accompanied me on many a trip across the state for my tennis matches.

Kathryn had an evolved sense of fairness. She was incredibly intelligent, generous, and unwavering in her emotional constancy. She did not provide a great deal of overt emotional support, but she did not require any from me either. Physical affection was displayed in what my sister and I called "mommy hugs" — a sort of pinch or pat that was more aggressive than it was comforting. What Kathryn lacked in affection she made up for in fun and play. She liked to have a good time, and while she had remained distant from Charlotte, she shared her desire for fun and companionship with me. While our friendship never went deep, it was wide. We were buddies, two Persephones in the meadow.

When Kathryn became ill, I lost almost everything about her that I knew. The hobbies and topics of conversation we always had in common became fewer and fewer until they eventually disappeared completely. The surface of this person I had known and connected with all my life slipped away, and what was left was an essence. Unlike Charlotte's experience, I found it was a quality I did not recognize and with which I could not connect ... except for her lightness of being. The happiness that I, unlike Charlotte, had experienced with my mother remained. Her laughter, which had been the hallmark of her being for me, continued to enliven our relationship.

Chapter Three

Dementia: A Sneaky Predator

Charlotte Parker

Family stories continue to be created throughout the process of dementia.

I can now look back and isolate the exact moment when I sensed the appearance of my mother's dementia, but in that moment no one knew or understood what was going on—least of all my mother and the medical professionals who were involved at the time. Shortly after the death of my father, Mom was diagnosed with a rare intestinal disorder called pseudomyxoma peritonei. The treatment required her to have an intestinal bypass surgery and the removal of an area in the small intestine essential for the metabolism of B vitamins. The B12 intrinsic factor plays an essential role in the proper functioning of the brain and spinal cord. As a result of my mother's bypass, her body could no longer metabolize this essential vitamin. Over the course of the next ten years, her body was slowly depleted of all B12. During this process of her nutritional depletion, her natural tendency for clutter and occasional forgetfulness became increasingly, and at times overwhelmingly, problematic.

The primary functions of B12 are the formation of red blood cells and the maintenance of a healthy nervous system. In order for the body's cells to function properly, B12 must be present in the tissue. If the body experiences a deficiency of B12, DNA production is interrupted and abnormal cells called megaloblasts develop which can result in pernicious anemia. The role of B12 in the nervous system is very important. An insulating fatty sheath comprised of complex proteins called myelin surrounds each of the nerves in our bodies. B12 is essential for the health and proper functioning of myelin. A prolonged B12 deficiency can lead to degenerative and irreversible neurological damage such as dementia.

Dementia is defined as a loss of mental functioning such as thinking, memory, and reasoning that is severe enough to interfere with a person's daily life. Dementia is actually not a disease in and of itself but rather a group of symptoms associated with other neurological diseases or conditions. The symptoms of dementia affect personality, mood, and behavior. Dementia patients often behave in a manner that is completely out of sorts with his or her "normal" personality. While dementia most often occurs over time, its predatory nature prevents most people from recognizing the symptoms of it until it is in its full-blown state. There were times, however, when my mother became so forgetful, that it was not only alarming to family members, but also frightening to my mother as well.

Dementia develops as a result of injury or disease to the area of the brain associated with learning, memory and/or decision making. This condition can lie dormant, waiting to be triggered by a trauma of some sort. A sudden onset of dementia can occur as a result of a high fever, or emotional or physical trauma. As a result of the B12 depletion caused from my mother's intestinal bypass, symptoms of dementia emerged so slowly they were not readily recognized.

When my mother was 72-years-old, she had a hysterectomy to remove cancer that had developed in her uterus. When she awoke from her surgery, she was a changed woman to me. It is this moment that was the beginning of my realization that something was wrong. Immediately, she began asking for the doctor, "When is the doctor coming?" over and over. Each time I reminded her that the doctor had already been by to visit her. I finally became concerned at her incessant inquiring and spoke to a nurse. The nurse assured me this was a normal aspect of recovering from anesthesia. However, the questioning expanded to many subjects and went on even as we drove home from the hospital several days post surgery. By this time, I was getting quite annoyed and angry with my mother. I misunderstood the relentless questioning as Mom's not paying attention to what I was saying. I believed at the time that she was absentmindedly ignoring my responses to her.

One specifically grueling line of questioning was brought on by the September 11, 2001 attack on the World Trade Center. If Mom asked me once, she asked me one hundred times, "What's that?" when the television aired the airplanes flying into the towers. Each timed I explained to her what had happened. This went on for weeks as I suffered through Mom's incessant line of repetitive questioning and her continuous surprise of hearing the news as if for the first time. In retrospect, her experience of the fall of the twin towers represented an external reflection of an internal collapse of Mom's rational faculties.

While at times it can be easy to accept forgetfulness, clutter, and the occasional repetitive questions as an inevitable aspect of aging, the experience of intensive repetition—in behavior, conversations, and questions—creates the awareness that something is simply not right. I found it impossible not to notice the perseveration, and my increasing anger in response became a kind of elephant in the room. The fact was that Mom had become a major disruption in my life. I was tired and stressed out in my attempts at support and care, at times not knowing if I was Demeter doing the burning or the one being burned. I moved through a kaleidoscope of progressive emotions: astonishment, annoyance, anger, then sadness and compassion and finally simply acceptance of the situation and our new reality.

My realization of the full impact and implications of Mom's condition occurred in moments tied to specific events in particular areas of her life. This experience was like the emergence of an underworld. One such occasion was especially telling.

Mom owned a beautiful mantel clock that had been in her home for over twenty years. At some point in the period subsequent to her surgery, she took her clock in for repair. Upon returning to retrieve it, she engaged in an argument with the repairman, convinced he was trying to give her a clock other than the one she had dropped off at his shop. She was so certain this clock did not belong to her that she brought me into the shop the next week. Much to the shop owner's relief, I immediately recognized the clock as belonging to my mother. Mom was visibly shaken by this experience. Little did we know at the time that a symbol of her future life had been enacted — the loss of familiarity and recognition of conventional Father Time. She was moving into her own world of time and space.

Mom was gradually losing the ability to remember the simplest tasks, but she also refused to allow me to take her to the doctor. For the most part, she was unaware that her mental functioning was deteriorating. If there is a silver lining to dementia, it is that the person is unaware of her deficiencies and is saved the conscious experience of frustration and embarrassment that characterize other illnesses. Specifically, Mom lost her capacity to work appliances and gadgets such as the microwave and toaster oven, and especially the television. Not long after returning from the hospital she forgot how to turn the television on and off. She could problem-solve to the extent that she would just unplug it from the wall and plug it back in when she wanted to watch television, but changing channels and operating the remote control or any of the control buttons was completely lost on her. Something she could do one day, she simply could not do the next. I wrote detailed instructions on paper and taped it to the television, but she was still confused.

Another clue that something was amiss was that Mom quit attending church. She had been an officer of her Sunday school class for many years. Her church community had been an important part of her life, and she simply discontinued attending without comment. When I asked her why she no longer attended church, she simply shrugged. She had no answer.

The straw that broke the camel's back came with tax season. Mom had been completing the taxes of my father's estate independently for over twenty years; however, her post-hysterectomy mental decline made the continuation of this independence impossible. In a very short time, she was rendered incapable of grasping even the most basic concepts of the tax preparation process. Important documents were scattered around the house amidst an ever-increasing clutter, which approached chaos. She had rapidly become disoriented in terms of understanding what information she needed to gather, where the documents had been placed, and why any of it was of any importance at all. What was most apparent was that she was completely unaware of her disorientation. Because the taxes needed to be completed upon a government-mandated deadline, I became involved in the process. At this time, I realized something was seriously wrong and beyond our control. I knew that whether she agreed with me or not, we needed to seek out the help of a specialist.

Finally, several months after her hysterectomy, I took my mother to see a neurologist. Upon meeting my mother, the doctor asked her to remember three words:

bell, book, and ball. He told her these words at the beginning of the meeting and asked her to recall them three minutes later. She not only could not recall the words, she had no memory that she was supposed to be remembering anything. The entire exercise was lost on her. He asked her several basic questions, all of which she was unable to accurately answer. She did not know who the President of the United States was, whether or not she had a gas or electric stove, or what year it was. Interestingly, she did know what year she was born, her home address, and her phone number. What I found to be most alarming was her lack of concern about this. She did not consider her inability to remember to be even remotely problematic.

A CAT scan revealed shrinkage in the frontal lobe of her brain, indicating a sign of frontal lobe dementia. The neurologist concluded that my mother was well into the stages of dementia and had probably been living with it for several years. From a mythological perspective, dementia — the sneaky predator that grabbed my mother after her hysterectomy — was a form of Hades taking her into his subterranean realm. What we did not realize was that the underworld for my mother was ultimately to be a place of profoundly positive feeling and well-being. A joyful place she had missed most of her adult life, and a place in which she became the queen.

Mom went on to live in her own home for another six years—much longer than the neurologist's suggested life expectancy based on how advanced the dementia was at the time of her diagnosis. With the assistance of hired caregivers, accompanied by my weekly visits, my mother was afforded a life of surprising independence— something that had always been of the utmost importance to her. While it was deeply distressing for those who loved my mother to witness the life-changing transformations caused by dementia, she herself was completely unaware of the changes she was experiencing.

Over time she lost the ability to focus on basic tasks such as grocery shopping, proper hygiene, and dressing. Her mind began to play tricks on her as she became convinced that people were stealing from her or that the people and actions on the television set were actually happening inside her home. She experienced a phase in which she wanted to listen to *The Three Tenors* album over and over and believed the concert was being held in her house just for her. She often thought there were other people in the house having parties upstairs. Her life became more otherworldly as the lines of her reality became increasingly blurred.

When my husband, Ron, traveled to Houston, he was fortunate to have Mom's house in which to stay over. This worked nicely for Mom as she enjoyed his company, and it gave me comfort knowing she had family looking after her. While I would come for the day, I rarely was able to stay the night since I had my business to take care of in Dallas. The arrangement worked nicely for us all. Ron slept in the upstairs bedroom that had once been mine as a teenager.

One evening, Mom came upstairs during a particularly deranged delusion. She pushed the door open and said, "You boys get out of here. I want you boys to get out of here. Now *Get!*" She went on hollering and demanding that he and "the boys" leave. Apparently the party was over, and it was time to go home. Ron awakened abruptly and was somewhat nervous knowing that she owned a handgun. He was not sure to what degree she might escalate and explained that "the boys" had already left to go to the "real party" where they could "really get drunk." This seemed to satisfy her, but on my next visit I did exchange the handgun for a starter pistol, which shoots only blanks.

Ron was very good at distracting Mom and understanding her reality in an empathic manner. On what was to be Mom's "last night out," we were having Christmas Eve dinner at my restaurant. I thought it might be risky to take her along since she often became agitated when in an unfamiliar setting. Sure enough, before the evening was half over, stimulated by even the small amount of wine she was allowed, Mom became quite angry and agitated. Not recognizing anyone at the table, she insisted that she did not belong there and that someone had better show her to the correct table. She got up and began moving around the restaurant. Ron quickly opened a side door leading from the dining room to an enclosed patio that served as a dining area and the entrance to the restaurant.

Once out in the patio, Mom banged on the table of a startled family and insisted that the gentleman at the table was the one she "should have been eating with all night." Ron readily agreed with her stating emphatically to one and all, "That's absolutely right, Kathryn! This is the man you should have been eating with." She was relieved, and paused for a moment, giving Ron a chance to change the subject.

"But you know what?" he asked.

"What?" she replied, ready for an argument.

"We might be in trouble," he responded, putting himself on her side of the conflict.

"We might?"

"Yes, somebody might be drunk!" he declared authoritatively.

"They might?" she asked, now somewhat alarmed.

"That's right, and you know what that means?"

"What?" she replied now with a genuinely felt need for help.

"That means we might be in trouble."

"We might!"

"Yes, and you know what that means?"

"What?"

"That means we better get out of here!"

"Oh."

"You know how we do that?"

"How?" she replied, now ready to accept

all the help she could get.

"Well, let's see. Usually the door is the best way out."

"It is?"

"Yes, and you know where the door is?"

"Where?"

"It looks like it's right behind you."

The two could now make their departure without any further complications, and Mom was gently taken back down to her world.

When Mom's first overnight caregiver Sandra began to stay the night in Houston, Mom began pulling some late night shenanigans with her. Sandra, an African-American woman from the deep south, was full of emotion, charisma and religion. When telemarketers called, Sandra would protect my mother by yelling at them in all earnestness, "Let loose the line Satan, let loose the line." Mom absolutely loved to be in her company. My mother always had great affection for the African-American culture, and she and Sandra developed a close relationship.

Because of their friendship, I was surprised when I noticed locks on the door to the bedroom that Sandra slept in. When I approached Sandra about the matter her eyes got very big as she explained how Mom would sneak up the stairs late at night while Sandra was sleeping and pinch her toes. She scared Sandra so badly the first couple of times she did it that Sandra could no longer fall asleep. She installed locks in order to get a bit of rest. Hades was gaining entrance to the house in more ways than one.

The transformation of my mother's mental health necessitated a journey we all — myself, my husband, sister, stepson, and her caregivers — embarked upon as we took over responsibility for her well-being. As the matriarch of our family changed, we were all transformed as well — emotionally and spiritually as individuals and as a family unit. As the fog of dementia slowly freed my mother of the constraints of the personality she had assumed and which we all knew, we came to know her in new and unique ways. We chose to live in her reality rather than attempt to force her to live in ours, and as a result, we became more playful and lived more in the present.

One evening when Ron and I were both staying the night at Mom's, she got up in the middle of the night to use the bathroom and became disoriented thinking the bathtub was the toilet. She fell into the bathtub and cracked her head. Mom cried out, and I rushed into the bathroom. I could not lift her out of the tub, so I cried out for Ron. He came staggering into the bathroom in his bathrobe and slippers, more asleep than awake. He proceeded to pick her up out of the tub, and as he did so, they found themselves holding on to each other, as if for mutual support. Mom's head was dripping blood to add to the spectacle, and I was taken aback to hear Ron's next words. "Well, Kathryn, if someone would just start the music, we can begin the dance." In fact, the dans macabre had already begun.

Virginia Parker

Family members each experience the loved one's dementia in their own unique way.

My perspective of our mother's condition is different from my sister's. I believe she became a child of the underworld long before her dementia set in overtly. From my earliest memory of our family home to my last memory, it was always a mess. My mother's natural propensity for clutter was something I always found embarrassing. While she was fastidious about her personal appearance and her automobile, our house and her children did not meet normal societal expectations. Until my sister and I were able to properly groom and dress ourselves, we remained as disheveled in appearance as the kitchen and den.

I do not believe my mother's lack of attention to our appearance could be considered negligent. I do not think it ever occurred to my mother to pay attention to the proper grooming of her children. Charlotte, as aware of social decorum as she was of my mother's beauty and self-care, learned early in her childhood to care for her own personal appearance. I also guess, as it truly is only a guess, that my mother's unusual propensity for clutter was the earliest sign of the dementia that would become my mother's reality later in life.

My sister and I grew up in the '50s when Donna Reed was the quintessential role model of the perfect mother and wife. While I was acutely aware of the clutter in our lives and embarrassed by Mother's lack of an attempt at creating the picture-perfect home, it did not occur to me until later in life that a complete dichotomy existed between our utterly messy home and our perfectly put together mother. While I was not conscious of this concept at the time, I have come to believe this disassociation of herself from her environment, a subtle form of alienating herself from everyone and everything, was the earliest manifestation of a neurological malfunction.

A traumatic event occurred in 1975 with the sudden and unanticipated death of my father. I was an accounting professor at Metropolitan State College of Denver and Charlotte was busy as the owner and operator of a new restaurant in Dallas. Our mother was going about life as usual at the family home in Houston when Happy suffered a fatal stroke while on business in Dallas. Once again, Charlotte was pulled center stage as we all suffered through this deeply sad time in our family history.

As the housemate, friend, and spouse of our mother, I believe Happy was the unknowing guardian protecting her from a decomposition that was manifesting itself through her inability to focus and the growing and constant appearance of household clutter. In my opinion, without the compensation of a companion in her life and deeply affected by the shock of his loss, my mother's natural propensity for clutter took on a deranged life of its own. With so much emptiness in her life, Kathryn slowly, over the course of the next twenty years, filled our family home from wall to ceiling, room by room with clutter. Without Happy, she had no containing structure.

Kathryn and Happy had maintained separate bedrooms for most of my life. I vaguely remember a time in my childhood when they shared a room, but for the majority of their marriage they maintained separate sleeping quarters. Happy snored with a bear-like quality that prevented anyone in close proximity from catching even a wink of sleep. And, to top that, he was a smoker who considered it his privilege to smoke in his personal space. Always years ahead of her time, our mother banished him from her room maintaining her own right to a good night's sleep and clean air to breathe. I suspect they both readily acknowledged the mutual benefit of this arrangement.

After his death, it was our father's room that was first filled to capacity with clutter. Next came the other family rooms. The den, the formal dining room, the kitchen, the living room, the stairs and on and on until there was nothing left but small pockets of space for my mother to sit in. Navigating this space required a periscope. One manifestation of Mom's extreme behavior was her propensity not to throw anything out, but rather to go shopping and buy new waste cans that would be consigned to the garage when full. Two rooms were spared the furnishings of Hades; our rooms— Charlotte's and mine—were left intact. On some unconscious level, Kathryn had attempted to fill the spaces, both physically and emotionally, that had once occupied her family life. She filled the house, and thereby her emotional self, to capacity. I often likened the process to a cancer of the house. Her grief had metastasized to every corner of her emotional and physical being.

I experienced this metastasizing of Kathryn's grief primarily on the phone. My trips back home to Houston were marked by notable changes in her mental well-being and confirmed by the deranged state of her cluttered surroundings. I witnessed the slipping away of the woman I knew and experienced a profound confusion and sadness by the woman who remained in her body. I turned to my sister for understanding. She turned to me for support. And in this way, our mother's illness brought us

together to develop a friendship and bond
we never realized was missing.

🌳

Chapter Four

Light in the Underworld
Understanding Dementia

Charlotte Parker

Be aware of the ever-growing, readily available, body of knowledge about dementia.

Contrary to common belief, dementia is not a normal part of the aging process. The presence of dementia symptoms is a clear sign of cognitive dysfunction. There are many diseases associated with dementia, some curable and some not. If dementia is caused by vitamin or hormonal deficiencies, as I believe to be the case of my mother, the symptoms of dementia may be resolved or greatly reduced if the underlying disease is treated. However, long-term deficiencies may cause irreparable damage.

A comprehensive evaluation of dementia symptoms is essential in order to seize the window of opportunity for treatment.

Unfortunately, in the case of my mother, the window of opportunity closed before we realized the truth of her condition. At the time of Mom's diagnosis, she had a total lack of B12 in her body. Through the lack of a proper medical diagnosis and follow-up treatment, my mother was well into dementia before anyone, her doctors included, understood the cause of her cognitive deterioration.

I believe my mother's journey into the depths of dementia began as a result of a misdiagnosed condition and an incorrect surgery. My mother was admitted to the hospital after suffering from ongoing stomach pain and unusual pelvic distension. She underwent an exploratory surgery in which the doctor discovered a large amount of a gelatinous substance. Unsure of what he had discovered, the doctor removed all of the foreign matter, and thinking it was a cancer associated with her intestines, also removed a large portion of her small intestines, including the areas responsible for the B12 intrinsic factor. The foreign matter was sent to pathology for testing and was eventually diagnosed as pseudomyxoma peritonei.

Pseudomyxoma peritonei (PMP) is a condition in which copious amounts of mucin are produced in the abdominal cavity. If left untreated, mucin will eventually build up to the point that it compresses vital internal structures such as the colon, the liver, and the kidneys. PMP is considered a cancer but unlike other cancers, it rarely spreads into the lymphatic system or through the bloodstream. While it is most commonly associated with cancer of the appendix, mucinous tumors can also grow in the ovaries. Symptoms include infertility, and, as in the case of my mother, abdominal or pelvic pain, distension, digestive disorders, weight changes, and increased girth. Diagnosis of PMP should always be confirmed through such diagnostic tests as CT scans and the evaluation of tumor markers.

The presence of PMP in my mother's abdomen was an indication of a leak in her appendix. The doctor should have cleaned out the gelatinous substance, washed out her intestines, and identified and repaired the leak. The removal of portions of her intestines was not only unnecessary, but ultimately proved to alter the course of my mother's life and the lives of all those who

Common Causes of Dementia

1. Degenerative Neurological Diseases
    *   Alzheimer's disease
    *   Parkinson's disease
    *   Huntington's disease
    *   Some types of multiple sclerosis

2. Vascular disorders

3. Multi-infarct dementia caused by multiple strokes in the brain

4. Traumatic brain injury caused by motor vehicle accidents, falls, etc.

5. Central nervous system infections
    *   Meningitis
    *   HIV
    *   Creutzfeldt-Jakob disease, a quickly progressing and fatal disease that is characterized by dementia and muscle twitching and spasm

6. Chronic alcohol or drug use

7. Depression

8. Certain types of hydrocephalus – an excess accumulation of fluid in the brain that can result from developmental abnormalities, infections, injury or brain tumors

Early Signs of Dementia

Cognitive Changes

Memory
Memory loss is the most common symptom of dementia. A person in the early stages of dementia has difficulty remembering recently learned information at an increasing rate of occurrence.

Familiar Tasks
Difficulty preparing meals, caring for basic hygiene, dressing oneself, and other day-to-day tasks are challenging or impossible to the person in the early phases of dementia.

Language
A person in the early stages of dementia may have a difficult time finding the right word, may use the wrong word, or even make up a word that is similar in sound to the word she wants to use. She may use unusual phrases, and may also find writing to be challenging.

Orientation
A person in the early stages of dementia may become confused in familiar

surroundings such as her own home, local market, etc.

Abstract Thinking
Mental tasks that require processing logical sequences such as following a conversation, writing a check, balancing the checkbook, etc. may become increasingly more challenging or impossible for the person in the early stages of dementia.

Judgment
The inability to make sound decisions regarding familiar tasks such as putting familiar objects away, dressing appropriately for the weather or social occasion, or putting things in nonsensical places (placing car keys in the refrigerator, etc.).

Behavior Changes

Personality
A notable shift in personality can be indicative of the early stages of dementia. For example, a typically cheerful person may become increasingly more agitated or easily angered.

Behavior or Mood

Dementias can cause severe and rapidly changing moods that can result in a vast range of emotions in a short period of time.

Energy

Early on-set dementia may cause a person to lose interest in activities that once brought happiness. She may sit for long periods of time watching television without indicating much interest. She may display a general sense of apathy towards life and loved ones.

Source: gilbertguide.com

love and care for her. The doctor took on the role of Hades to my mother's Persephone.

As a consequence of losing a significant portion of her small intestines, my mother lost the ability to metabolize and store B12 in her body. Her doctors failed to, or did not know to, prescribe supplemental B12 injections, without which my mother's body became depleted of B12 within the following decade. A simple monthly B12 injection might have prevented my mother from slipping into the altered dimensions of dementia. Throughout the tens years of exhausting her B12 supply, my mother gradually slipped into dementia. When she subsequently underwent a hysterectomy, she awakened to a new reality—a reality in which she was too far gone to change. She had already taken the pomegranate seed and no reversal was possible.

Understanding the various causes of dementia is the most important component of preventing this debilitating disorder. There is much truth in the saying, "Hindsight is 20/20." Fortunately, we can borrow the 20/20 lens of those who have gone before us to view our own circumstances and perhaps make more educated decisions.

Types of Dementia

There are two broad categories of dementia with each category affecting a specific part of the brain: the cortical dementias and the subcortical dementias.

Cortical causes of dementia result from a disorder affecting the cerebral cortex. The cerebral cortex is the outer layer of the brain that plays an important role in cognitive abilities such as memory and language. Subcortical dementias result from a dysfunction in the parts of the brain that are beneath the cortex. Usually, the forgetfulness and language difficulties that are characteristic of cortical dementias are not present with subcortical dementias. People with subcortical dementias — such as Parkinson's disease, Huntington's disease and AIDS dementia complex — show changes in their speed of thinking, as well as their ability to initiate activities.

Non-Treatable Forms of Dementia

- Alzheimer's disease is the most common form of dementia. Alzheimer's is a progressive, incurable and ultimately fatal brain disease affecting as many as five million Americans. Alzheimer's destroys brain cells resulting in impaired cognitive processing which impact memory, thinking, and behavior. The cognitive damage eventually becomes so severe the individual is no longer capable of continuing to work or enjoy lifelong hobbies. Alzheimer's is currently the sixth-leading cause of death in the United States. *Source: alz.org*

• Vascular dementia is caused by reduced blood flow to various parts of the brain. Vascular dementia is a "catch all" term used to describe impairments in cognitive function caused by problems in the blood vessels that supply nutrients to the brain. In some cases of vascular dementia, a blood vessel may become completely blocked resulting in a stroke, which may or may not result in dementia. Vascular dementia can also occur as a result of narrowing blood vessels in the brain, which reduces the necessary amount of blood flow to the brain. Vascular dementia affects from 1 to 4 percent of people over the age of 65. *Source: mayoclinic.com*

• Dementia occurs in approximately 20 percent of people with Parkinson's disease and usually not until the age of 70.

In general, there is a 10 to 15 year period between a Parkinson's diagnosis and the onset of dementia, which typically occurs years after the motor skills begin to be affected. Signs of dementia in Parkinson's patients include: memory problems, distractibility, slowed thinking, disorientation, confusion, moodiness, and a general lack of motivation. *Source: helpguide.org*

- AIDS dementia complex (ADC) is also known as HIV-associated dementia (HAD). Most AIDS-related illnesses are caused by other infections such as bacteria, fungi, and other viruses, but ADC is one of the only illnesses that can be caused directly by HIV as a result of the virus permeating the brain. Twenty to 35 percent of all HIV-positive people will eventually develop some symptoms of ADC. *Source: aidsmeds.com*

- Creutzfeldt-Jakob disease (CJD) became associated with mad cow disease in the 1990s when beef consumers in the United Kingdom developed a form of the disease—variant CJD (vCJD)—after eating meat from cattle suspected of having mad cow disease. However, "classic" Creutzfeldt-Jakob disease has not been linked to beef contaminated with mad cow disease. This rapidly progressing, degenerative brain disorder eventually leads to dementia and is fatal. *Source: mayoclinic.com*

Treatable Causes of Dementia

In theory, if the following causes of dementia are treated within an adequate time frame, the resulting dementia may be reversed or significantly halted.

- Alcohol related dementia is caused by damage to multiple nerves in both the central nervous system (brain and spinal cord) and the peripheral nervous system (the rest of the body). The cause of this type of dementia is simply malnutrition, especially a lack of vitamin B-1 (thiamine), a common result of habitual alcohol use. Alcohol related dementia involves an impairment of memory and intellect/cognitive skills such as problem solving or learning, along with multiple symptoms of nerve damage. A common symptom of alcohol related dementia is confabulation (fabrication) in which the person fabricates detailed stories about experiences or situations to cover gaps in memory. Treatment for alcohol related dementia involves seeking professional assistance in eliminating alcohol from the diet, accompanied with a nutritional diet under the care of a professional nutritionist to replenish nutrients in the body and brain.

• Brain tumors can cause symptoms of dementia, but when operable, this type of dementia is treatable.

• A subdural hematoma occurs when blood collects or pools within an area of the head, between the brain and the skull, leading to a compression of the affected brain area. The pressure resulting from the collection of blood — the hematoma — creates symptoms commonly exhibited as dementia. Attributed to a variety of circumstances, the subdural hematoma is usually the result of a head injury, but can be attributed to viral and bacterial infections as well. If left untreated, patients suffer a progressive deterioration in mental capacity. A subdural hematoma is easily diagnosed with an MRI scan.

This form of dementia is treated usually with a simple, although risky, surgical procedure.

- Normal pressure hydrocephalus is a brain disorder that occurs as a result of blocked cerebrospinal fluid. A clear fluid called cerebrospinal fluid (CSF) surrounds the brain and spinal cord and is produced and stored in brain cavities called ventricles. CSF circulates around the brain, moving from ventricle to ventricle. The purposes of the fluid are to cushion and protect the brain and spinal cord, to supply them with nutrients, and to remove some of their waste products. Any excess fluid drains away from the brain and is absorbed by other tissue. If the ventricles hold too much CSF they become enlarged in order to accommodate the extra fluid and as a result begin to press on different parts of the brain.

- Normal pressure hydrocephalus (NPH) usually occurs in older people over the age of sixty years. NPH develops slowly over time as a result of slow CSF drainage and a gradual build-up of excess fluid.

The ventricles slowly become enlarged resulting in a gradual increase in brain pressure. The gradual increase in pressure can cause a slow onset of dementia symptoms. The dementia symptoms of NPH are similar to those of Alzheimer's and Parkinson's diseases; however, unlike Alzheimer's disease and Parkinson's disease, NPH may be reversed with appropriate treatment. *Source: WebMd.com*

• Metabolic disorders, such as a vitamin B12 deficiency can cause dementia but may be reversible if treated properly and timely. Vitamin B12 (cobalamin) is a vital water-soluble vitamin that accumulates in the body and is stored in the liver, kidney, and other body tissues. Because of the way B12 is stored in the body, a deficiency may not manifest itself until after five years or as long as ten years. Vitamin B12 functions as a methyl donor and works with folic acid in the synthesis of DNA and red blood cells and is vitally important in maintaining the health of the insulation sheath (myelin sheath) that surrounds the body's nerve cells.

A B12 deficiency often manifests itself first in the development of neurological dysfunction that is almost indistinguishable from senile dementia and Alzheimer's disease. However, these symptoms may be reversible through effective supplementation.

The amount of vitamin B12 needed by the body is very small, probably only about two micrograms or two millionths of a gram per day. However, the human body does not readily absorb B12, and therefore, a larger quantity is necessary in order to supply the body and brain with enough of this nutrient to function properly. Many elderly people become B12 deficient because their production of the intrinsic factor necessary to absorb the vitamin from the small intestine declines rapidly with age.

Injections of vitamin B12 are often prescribed to elderly people or people whom, for various reasons, are not able to metabolize B12 through oral supplements.

- Hypothyroidism — a condition in which the thyroid gland does not produce sufficient hormone production — can result in apathy or depression that mimics dementia. Proper diagnosis and treatment of the thyroid may reverse the disorder.

- Hypoglycemia, a condition in which there is not enough sugar in the bloodstream, can cause confusion or personality changes that mimic dementia. Proper treatment of hypoglycemia can reverse the dementia.

Chapter Five

Marking the Descent
Phases of Dementia

Charlotte Parker

During the difficult times remember that a sweet, compliant person will eventually emerge.

There are many phases of dementia. Not everyone who suffers from dementia will experience every phase, but caregivers should be aware of each phase in order to meet the person's needs compassionately and knowledgeably. The patterns of behavior and the speed in which an individual's abilities deteriorate vary from person to person. Sometimes a caregiver will notice a significant deterioration from morning to evening, some changes occur from one day to the next, other changes are slower and may occur over weeks, months, or even years. The pattern is not predictable. The only thing that is predictable is that mental and physical capacities will deteriorate. The many transformations of dementia are generally classified into three phases: early, moderate, and severe.

Early Phase of Dementia

As in the case with our mother, the early phase of dementia is rarely recognized. Friends, family, and the dementia sufferer herself may pass off the signs as unfortunate but inevitable characteristics of aging, too much work, or perhaps stress. The following are signs that dementia may be present:

- A general lack of enthusiasm or an overall sense of apathy

- A loss of interest in hobbies or activities

- An unwillingness to try new things

- An inability to adapt to change

- Tendency to demonstrate poor judgment or decision making

Baby Kathryn Foote, 1918

Kathryn Foote, 1939

Kathryn & Jim (Happy) Parker, 1960s

Wedding Portrait, August 20, 1943

Kathryn Parker, Mid-1990s

Virgina Parker, Irene McDaniel, & Kathryn, 85th Birthday

Charlotte Parker & Bum, White Rock Stables, 2009

Jim Parker & Kathryn Foote, WWII

Alfred, Mary Louise & Kathryn Foote, Early 1920s

Kathryn & Baby Virginia, Early 1949

Virgina Parker, 2009

Kathryn, The Career Woman

Kathryn at Lone Camp Ranch, 2003

Halloween Party, 2005

Kathryn & College Roommate Marguerite Nichols, 2005

Kathryn & Grandson of Caregiver Viginia Vasquez, 2007

- Slow to grasp complex ideas

- Slow to accomplish routine jobs

- Belief that people are stealing from them

- Self-centered and less concerned with the other people's feelings

- Forgetful of details of recent events

- Repeat themselves and easily get "off track" in conversations

- Easily irritated or upset if they fail at a task

- Experience difficulty handling money

Whether our mother's dementia was caused by the pseudomyxoma peritonei as I believe, or rooted in a lifelong emotional disorder that manifested itself as dementia after our father died, as my sister believes, or perhaps a combination of the two, Mom began to display these telltale signs in the late 70s. With Happy's sudden passing in

1975 and her intestinal bypass surgery occurring shortly thereafter, it is impossible to pinpoint the exact moment this early phase set in. Because we all three lived in different cities many of these symptoms became evident to my sister and me through phone conversations with Mom.

Mom was an avid gardener. For as long I can remember, my mother sought refuge in the garden. She created lavish and well organized gardens and could easily spout off the Latin and common names of all her plants. Under her care, the garden never gathered the clutter that characterized the inside of the house. However, her garden bore witness to her disease as it progressed in its early stages. Weeds began to make an appearance, and the organization of plants slowly began to mirror Mom's mental state as they morphed into clusters of randomly and illogically placed plants. Her beautiful garden began to take on the same cluttered, under worldly quality as the house. Demeter, goddess of the harvest, was losing her hold on the harvest.

Housekeepers who had worked for our mother for years voiced their concerns about accusations of their stealing while Mom maintained her certainty of their guilt.

Money became increasingly more challenging for our mother. A marathon shopper, she went from "shopping till she dropped" to never shopping at all. Finding the concept of money too challenging or confusing, she chose to give up an activity that had brought her so much fun her entire life.

Moderate Phase of Dementia

Once the dementia has moved into the moderate, or middle, phase, the signs become more apparent and disabling. The following signs are indicative the dementia has progressed beyond its early stage:

- Able to remember the distant past with some confusion, but has difficulty remembering recent events

- Experiences confusion regarding time and place

- May become lost when away from familiar surroundings

- May forget the names of family and friends

- May confuse one family member or friend with another

- May forget to turn the stove or oven on while cooking

- May wander the streets at night becoming lost and disoriented

- May behave inappropriately (i.e., going outdoors dressed in pajamas)

- May see or hear things that are seemingly not there

- May become repetitive

- May become unconcerned with hygiene and eating

- May become easily angered or upset

This moderate phase of dementia is very disheartening for family. In retrospect, the early phase of dementia becomes clearer at this time as the pieces of the past start coming together and the unusual or "out of character" behavior begins to make more sense.

🌳

I began weekly visits to Houston in 1995 shortly after Mom had her hysterectomy and the fullness of her dementia had set in. Her garden, which had already transitioned from a state of order to a state of chaos, was still a source of comfort to her.

She experienced a period in which she was convinced that the leaves in her garden were highly valuable. Her caregiver and I found carefully placed leaves throughout the house and in most of her personal items. She placed them in her wallet, her pockets, in drawers, and anywhere else she thought might be a safe place to keep these precious items. I experienced a profound sadness during this time. I thought about other people witnessing this behavior and what they would think about this deranged woman collecting leaves as though they were literally gold coins. Mom loved the outdoors. She loved nature and the beauty of the earth. I recognized this action of collecting leaves as a confused and child-like association to something she had always loved dearly. Once again, Demeter, goddess of the harvest, was searching for her lost children.

Mom had always taken great pride in her appearance. She had closets and closets full of matching outfits with coordinating handbags, shoes, and accessories. As her dementia progressed, she lost her ability to dress herself. She experienced a total confusion regarding the appropriateness and purpose of particular items. One day she came out of her room dressed for our weekly errands to the grocery store, the bank, and lunch wearing her blouse as pants. She had put her legs through the arms of her top and pronounced herself ready to go. There comes a time when one can find the humor in this disease, Baubo flashing herself to Demeter, but in this moderate phase of dementia, laughter can be difficult.

Communicating on the telephone, still at this time very much a necessary way to stay in touch with my mother, became increasingly more challenging. Using cordless phones was next to impossible, as she could never remember where the handset was located. Although Mom had always been quite a mechanically inclined engineer in her understanding of technology, she suddenly became terrified of electricity and frightened by any loose wires. The only phone she was able to use was the kitchen wall phone — the old model that hung on the wall with a long cord running to the receiver. There were many times she would call me in need of assistance in finding something, and I would give her explicit instructions: *First put the phone down, then walk into the kitchen, next open the cabinet door, etc.* If I missed one step in the series of instructions (such as *put the phone down*) she would become very confused. However, she was exceptionally good at following each step exactly as I presented them. The challenge was for me to think through each small step without making any assumptions. For example, I would need to say, "Open the cabinet door," rather than, "Go to the cabinet." It was a great lesson in patience, as well as managing minute details. I was conscious to keep my sense of humor about these situations, which was quite honestly the only way to get through this phase of Mom's illness.

As Mom's fear of electricity progressed, she began cutting wires to the few electrical items she still understood how to operate. When I came to her house one morning and found the electric burners cut off the stovetop, I knew Mom was in danger. She could no longer live alone. I had to make arrangements for round the clock care.

Severe Phase of Dementia

During the final, or severe, phase of dementia, the person requires continuous care twenty-four hours a day. At this stage, she is not only a danger to herself, but is also incapable of self-care. The following signs suggest the dementia sufferer has reached the late stages of illness:

- Unable to remember anything that has just happened (i.e., cannot remember the meal that was just eaten)

- Loses the ability to understand or use speech

- Becomes incontinent

- No longer recognizes friends and family

- Can no longer eat, wash, bathe, or use the toilet without assistance

- Unable to recognize common objects

- May become aggressive if they feel threatened or closed in

- Loses the ability to walk

My mother is blessed to have a loyal team of caregivers who are like family to her. They love her and care for her with the same tenderness and compassion as they would their own child. In all the years she has remained in need of in-home care, not one of her caregivers has ever called in sick. So loyal are her caregivers that two of them drive from Houston to Dallas every other week to be with her for an extended five-day period.

By the time I moved Mom to Dallas, she was severely demented but still quite mobile. She could talk, but she did not always have an understanding of what she was saying or what others were saying to her. The weekend of her move, I brought mother and her caregiver, Ana, to her new home. We all spent the night at my house that first night to await the delivery of her household items the next day. This was the first time Mother had slept away from her home in almost a year. She was tucked away in the guest bedroom positioned in the front of the house, while Ana was stationed in another room.

Ana and I woke early the next morning and visited over coffee in the kitchen waiting for Mom to wake up and the movers to arrive. We knew it would be a busy time, and we were enjoying our coffee and procrastinating before the start of what would surely be an exhausting day. We concluded at about ten o'clock that we should wake my mother and get her ready for the day. Ana went to the bedroom and quickly returned notably alarmed. Mom was missing.

I found myself re-enacting Demeter in her search for Persephone as Ana and I embarked on our long journey to find my "daughter." We searched the house from top to bottom calling her name. We looked through every closet, under the beds, in the bathrooms, and anywhere else we thought she might have wandered. We combed the neighborhood calling her name. It was a chilly fall morning. Leaves and acorns were scattered about the lawns on our block. I felt hopeless as I imagined my mother cold, scared, lost, and incapable of seeking help or finding her way home.

Eventually we had no choice but to call the police. They arrived promptly and asked me a series of questions, all of which I was unable to answer. What was she wearing?

When did she go missing? Why would she leave?

Shortly after the police reported her missing, they received a call from the county hospital. I rushed over to retrieve her from the emergency room. She was filthy, barefoot, and exhausted. She had been picked up by a police officer at the end of my street. Unable to identify herself and disoriented with her surroundings, all she could tell the police officer was that she lived in Houston. She said she was visiting her daughter but either refused to tell my name or could not remember my name. She had arrived at the hospital barefoot with acorns stuck between her toes shivering in the cold wearing only the pink pajamas she had worn to bed.

The hospital staff had run a battery of tests on her. Not knowing anything about her, they had tested her for every street drug as well as the usual run of stress tests. Not surprisingly, her blood pressure was high but other than that she seemed fine.

I addressed the police officer who had been watching over my mother and thanked him for his kindness. As we were walking out the door Mom looked back at the officer and said, "You know what you have been acting like. You are not a gentleman!" Mom was in no mood to be thankful for the kindness of strangers.

As we rode home from the hospital, Mom looked over at me and proclaimed with complete seriousness, "I have never been so tired in my life." My thoughts were turning to the comment the officer had stated to me, "Lady, you need to be more careful with your mother. This is just the *first* time." I vowed to myself then and there that this would be the first and last time I ever had to go in search of my mother.

While many abilities are lost as dementia progresses, the individual does retain his or her sense of touch and hearing, as well as the ability to respond emotionally. Once Mom moved into her new home in Dallas, her certainty that people were stealing from her increased. She thought there were people on the second floor (the house only has one floor) who were taking things from her. As was the case in her old home, she believed they were having parties and carrying on into the wee hours of the morning. Sometimes she told me about these delusions as if they had happened at some point earlier in the day or perhaps in the evening, and other times she would tell me as though they were happening at that very moment. At this stage of her dementia, I had learned there was no point in arguing with her. I stepped into her reality and would often become highly absorbed in the drama that was playing out in her head.

Sometimes I believe she knew she was making up stories and was humored by my willingness to indulge her. One day I asked her if she had any secrets. She said she did. She told me an elaborately fabricated story about boyfriends she had been involved with before and during her marriage. She told me with a deadpan expression that my father had been a black man. Often her stories were the by-product of delusions, some of which could be unnerving and scary, and others that were wildly entertaining. I remain consistent in my willingness to be there with her, wherever she is and in whatever dimension she resides. I stay by her side and comfort her in the scary times, and laughed with her in the joyful. I have learned that Hades, the devil, and Baubo, the clown, go hand in hand in the as one journeys into the depths of dementia.

Sundowners Syndrome

Sundowners Syndrome, also called Sundowning Syndrome, is a common syndrome affecting dementia patients. While not all dementia patients experience this phenomenon, most do. My mother experienced this syndrome after she moved into the "severe" phase of dementia and was already living in her new home.

Sundowner Syndrome is a bit of a medical mystery. What is agreed upon about this syndrome is that for some reason, dementia patients experience an added layer of confusion. In the late afternoon, or at sundown, there is a shift in the individual's understanding of her current reality that results in disorientation and anxiety with regard to her circumstances. Paranoid delusions may appear or increase. Restlessness and wandering are also common, but the behaviors associated with this syndrome are highly individualized.

Some doctors believe that the accumulation of sensory stimulation experienced throughout the day begins to overwhelm and cause stress to the dementia patient by evening, while others speculate that the syndrome is caused by hormonal imbalances that occur at night. Still others insist that the onset of symptoms is a result of simple fatigue from the day or perhaps anxiety associated with poor nighttime vision. Scientific studies do support the theory that the symptoms have something to do with darkness. Doctors have noted that the symptoms tend to subside within an hour of the return of daylight. There is also a correlation with Seasonal Affective Disorder (SAD), which is believed to cause depression in the winter due to the shorter periods of sunlight.

Mom began proclaiming her desire to "go home" every day at five o'clock in the afternoon regardless of whether it was dark or not. She believed we were in a public space, such as a school or a library, that closed at five o'clock and that we needed to be out before we became locked in for the evening. She demonstrated this behavior for so many years that she had us all programmed for our five o'clock exit. She would adamantly proclaim that we had to leave. She became increasingly agitated if we argued with her and attempted to explain that she was already home.

One day I simply said, "Okay Mom, let's go home. Get your purse, and let's go home." She retrieved her purse, and we walked out the front door. We went all the way around the house and re-entered the front door. She was home. By indulging her behavior and stepping into her reality, we saved ourselves hours of arguing, and we saved her great stress and anxiety.

Sundowner Syndrome is a normal part of the dementia experience, but there are ways to minimize its impact on the patient. The following guidelines may be of assistance:

- Maintain a structured daily routine. By following a structured routine that the person can rely on, the number of decisions the person needs to make in a day is decreased, which may assist in reducing anxiety.

- Simplify the person's world. As her world becomes more difficult to understand, everyday tasks become increasingly more overwhelming. Minimize the number of decisions she must make in a day. If the person is still able to dress herself, reduce the number of clothes in the closet to two or three items. If she is able to feed herself, provide as few options as possible. Reduce as many stressors as possible. Understand that physical comfort is paramount to the person with dementia. Ensuring physical comfort will greatly reduce stressors in her daily life.

- Turn the interior lights on prior to dusk. The increased light may assist in reducing disorientation.

- Be cognizant of environmental stressors. Like a child, the dementia sufferer is dependent on the caregiver to ensure a stable and safe environment. People with dementia may become concerned if they lose sight of their caregiver. The caregiver's tone of voice, facial expressions, and body movements are all forms of communication that provide either comfort or stress. Be conscious of the message being sent. Quietly tend to routine rituals.

- Plan activities for the late afternoon and early evening that are relaxing and allow the individual to expend her energy in a controlled manner. Offer reassurance if the person becomes agitated. A gentle touch or a kind conversation may calm the patient and let her know she is loved and appreciated.

• Lastly, indulge the behavior. The person with dementia is as certain of her reality as the caregiver is of her own.

Virginia Parker

Confrontation is useless; acceptance is key.

Because Charlotte has managed our mother's care through every phase of her dementia, I have benefited tremendously from her hard-earned understanding of the process. I experienced an instant, pivotal epiphany when Charlotte once said to me, "It's not about you, Virginia. It's about Mom." I understood then that regardless of whether I am unable or unwilling to participate in effective fantasy role-play with Kathryn, I understood that nothing good would come from my being confrontational about what is and is not reality.

My advice to others faced with parental dementia is this: When dealing with an irreversible loss of function, don't waste time on what is not recoverable and focus instead on what is left. For me, what remained intact in Kathryn was her joy. We embraced Baubo and Iambe.

Chapter Six

The Duality of the Mother Archetype

Charlotte Parker

Mothers become daughters, and
daughters become mothers.

Demeter is a complex and multi-faceted goddess. As the goddess of the harvest and the four seasons, she represents life from the tiniest kernel to the fullness of the harvest and the barren winter to the life-producing spring. Demeter is Life in its full cycle, but there is a duality to Demeter common to Greek gods. She is both Mother and Child: The power she holds over the harvest is lost during fallow months, and she must spend these days in other pursuits. As Mother she harnesses her nurturing power, but as the Child she lets the earth go. Demeter mourns as she roams the earth seeking her lost daughter in much the same way a child despairs in abandonment when she has lost her mother. The experience of the emotion is one and the same — a rejoining of the oneness of the Mother-Child connection. Demeter and Persephone are essentially one, and when they are no longer together, they each experience a physical, spiritual, and mental disconnect requiring a journey to reunite.

Demeter embodies Carl Jung's descriptive qualities of the mother archetype. In his essay, *The Psychological Aspects of the Mother Archetype*, Jung explains, "The qualities associated with it [the mother archetype] are maternal solicitude and sympathy; the magic authority of the female; any helpful instinct or impulse; all that is benign, all that cherishes and sustains, and fosters growth and fertility. The place of magic transformation and rebirth, together with the underworld and its inhabitants, are presided over by the mother." The magical maternal qualities did not appear in my mother until the dementia began to break down the walls that had been so rigidly built up in her psyche.

Caring for a parent with dementia is much like caring for a baby, except with a parent there is a lifetime of emotional and spiritual baggage to sift through. My sister and I had on many occasions commented with satisfaction that we had managed to make our way through our lives without the interruption and complications associated with parenting a child. What we did not know until we embarked on the journey of caring for our mother is that along with the heartache and tears that caring for someone who depends on you for her well-being brings, it also brings with it a beautiful sense of purpose and joy.

Dementia, like Hades, creeps into a person's life with no warning. By the time a diagnosis is made, the individual is usually well into the stages of the disorder. By its very nature, this symptomatic condition cheats everyone — the individual suffering from dementia, as well as her friends and family — from going through the emotional preparation necessary for a life-altering experience. The sooner that we, as caregivers, were able to acknowledge that all the baggage we had carried as daughters no longer served us, the easier our new role as the caregivers became. What helped us most was the realization that our mother was now mythically in a new world.

When my mother was first diagnosed with dementia, I was at the peak of my career as a successful co-owner of one of Dallas' most popular wine bistros. I had worked diligently my entire life to create a life of distinction, and I was in full bloom. I divided my time between the restaurant, my real estate business, my art studio, my horses, my husband, and my stepson. I was busy, and I loved it. My restaurant received national recognition, an upscale department store carried my artwork, and my leisure time was filled with creative people and creative activities. I had created a life that read like a novel. People were impressed by my accomplishments, and I was even impressed. Of course, the one person I desperately wanted to notice these accomplishments never outwardly seemed to care.

I spent my life trying to get my mother's attention. From my perspective, nothing I did seemed grand enough to warrant comment from her. When the roles reversed and all the inhibitions, fears, insecurities, pride, expectations, and countless other childlike aspects that comprised her hidden personality emerged out of her dementia, I became the center of her universe. In caring for my mother, I finally felt important to her. The love she gave me dissolved the past hurt.

Jung explains this interesting and complex duality of the mother archetype as demonstrated in Demeter and Persephone's (Kore's) relationship.

Demeter and Kore, mother and daughter, extend the feminine consciousness both upwards and downwards. They add an "older and younger," "stronger and weaker" dimension to it and widen out the narrowly limited conscious mind bound in space and time, giving it intimations of a greater and more comprehensive personality which has a share in the eternal course of things. We can hardly suppose that myth and mystery were invented for any conscious purpose; it seems much more likely that they were the involuntary revelation of a psychic, but unconscious, pre-condition. The psyche pre-existent to consciousness (e.g., in the child) participates in the maternal psyche on the one hand, while on the other it reaches across to the daughter psyche. We could therefore say that every mother contains her daughter in herself and every daughter her mother, and that every woman extends backwards into her mother and forwards into her daughter. This participation and intermingling give rise to that peculiar uncertainty as regards time: a woman lives earlier as a mother, later as a daughter. The conscious experience of these ties produces the feeling that her life is spread out over generations — the first step towards the immediate experience and conviction of being outside time, which brings with it a feeling of immortality. The individual's life is elevated into a type, indeed it becomes the archetype of woman's fate in general. This leads to a restoration or apocatastasis of the lives of her ancestors, who now, through the bridge of the momentary individual, pass down into the generations of the future. An experience of this kind gives the individual a place and a meaning in the life of the generations, so that all unnecessary obstacles are cleared out of the way of the life-stream that is to flow through her. At the same time the individual is rescued from her isolation and restored to wholeness.

All ritual preoccupation with archetypes ultimately has this aim and this result. [C. G. Jung, *The Archetypes and the Collective Unconscious*, 2nd ed. New York, Bollingen Foundation Inc., 1959, p. 188.]

Dementia brought a death to the mother of my childhood. However, through dementia my mother experienced a re-birthing in the form of her daughter self. In that experience, I gained a re-birthing myself in consciously accepting the role of mother. I simultaneously became a mother and found my mother in the mysteries of this disease.

The discovery of my new connection with Mom, again without my full realization, was accomplished with the help of a spirit guide. In the early stages of my mother's dementia, I became increasingly interested in the Virgin of Guadalupe, also known as Our Lady of Guadalupe. This is unusual from a Baptist woman such as myself, but I did not question the pull that I felt from her. The Virgin first appeared to a villager, Juan Diego, in central Mexico at the Hill of Tepeyac in the form of an apparition. She came to be a national icon, as well as incorporated into spiritual and religious ceremonies and beliefs. Before Mom moved to Dallas, I unconsciously began filling my life with this mother figure that represented the very duality I was experiencing in my own life. Mosaic figures I was creating in my artwork took on the aspect of the Virgin, and she made her presence known as I placed them throughout my house.

Our Lady of Guadalupe is often considered as one and the same with the Virgin Mother of Christ who is both Mother and Child. There is a flow in how the Mother and Child both fulfill their life purpose. In the case of the Virgin Mother, her purpose is to bring the Child into the world so that she, and the world at large, might be saved. Demeter must bring Persephone into the world so that she might lose her, and therefore bring balance and harmony (i.e., seasons) into the world upon her return.

My experience with my mother embodies the human aspect of these divinity stories. My mother brought me into the world and lost herself in the role of motherhood. Through a strange and unexpected initiation, we found ourselves in one another. This archetypal process lives on in our lives as it does in the image of the Virgin Mother.

Chapter Seven

A Temple for Our Mother

Charlotte Parker

"I ardently desire a temple be built here for me where I will show and offer all my love, my compassion, my help and my protection to the people. I am your Mother, the Mother of all who live united in this land, and of all mankind, of all those who love me, of those who cry to me, of those who have confidence in me. Here I will hear their weeping and their sorrows, and will remedy and alleviate their sufferings, necessities and misfortunes."
- The Virgin of Guadalupe to Juan Diego

For several years after my mother's diagnosis, I made a weekly pilgrimage to Houston. My husband and I caught the first flight out of Dallas to Houston at 7am, arriving in Houston at 8am. We then picked up a rental car, maneuvered through rush hour traffic, and after dropping my husband off at the office I arrived at Mom's by 9:30 in the morning.

Every Thursday was the same. I spent the first hour searching through the house collecting all the mail that had been randomly strewn about the home. I drove Mom to the bank, then on to the grocery store, out to lunch, and then back to the office to pick my husband up. My mother was cantankerous and ornery at that stage of her illness, and I only fueled it by arguing with her and trying to "talk some sense" into her. I flew home each Thursday evening utterly exhausted. I felt unappreciated, because I was unappreciated. I had not yet realized that my mother was incapable of feeling gratitude.

Each week I noticed my mother losing more of her ability to function independently, and as a result I began to hold her less accountable. The more abilities she lost, the more compassion I found within myself. She lost the ability to drive, to dress, to write a check, and eventually to sign her name. I began to realize that I was losing my mother, and the resentment of not being appreciated was replaced with a deep mourning.

Many times during my mother's dementia we experienced situations that worked out so serendipitously it was as if a form of divine intervention was at play. From 1995 through most of 2001, I maintained my weekly travel schedule to Houston to care for my mother. Occasionally I drove to Houston to bring Mom back for a weekend stay in Dallas for holidays, birthdays, and other special occasions. On August 27, 2001, I pulled out of my driveway heading for Houston. It was my birthday weekend, and I wanted Mom to be in Dallas with me to celebrate. Just as I pulled out of the driveway I noticed the sun shining brilliantly on my Lady of Guadalupe garden statue. I got goosebumps at the sight of her beauty, and thought, "It is a good sign. This will be a great trip!" I headed off feeling upbeat and enthusiastic about Mom's visit.

Road trips are always enjoyable as they allow time for the mind to relax and thoughts to wander. I remember thinking to myself how convenient it would be to purchase a house in my neighborhood for Mom. The trips to Houston were taking their toll on me, and I worried about her more and more. She needed round the clock care, and I needed the peace of mind that would only come with having her closer.

I picked her up in the late morning and drove back to Dallas on that same day. At some point during the day, the house directly across the street from mine was placed on the market. Less than two weeks later on September 11, 2001, the twin towers in New York City were demolished changing all of our lives. There is no way I could have maintained my travel schedule to Houston during those early post 9/11 days. The travel was already taxing enough on me, but the heightened security would have imposed an impossible time-constraint. We made an offer on the home immediately, and Mom was in Dallas less than two months later.

My mother's home is very otherworldly. Stepping into her house is entering a realm outside of time and space. Everything is in order, taking place at its own pace, with all focus on Mom. Her home is a place of healing, and a member of the small community of caregivers is always available. Yet, the space itself, with its atmosphere of laughter and good feeling also has a rejuvenating effect on everyone who enters. The home that many might refer to as a "sick house," instead is a temple of hope and happiness.

My mother's caregivers are an effective social and spiritual network for my family and me. Each of these steadfast women touches our lives in their own special way. Their dedication to my mother is second only to their own internal, friendly competition to "out do" one another in their caregiving. These women are another example of the larger than life, great Mother at work in our lives as one by one each woman continuously steps forward to take her place in my mother's care.

Ana is a naturalized U.S. citizen from El Salvador. She speaks English as a second language, but not very well which has made communicating with her over the years a dramatic act of charades and monosyllabic explanations. Yet, we always manage to understand each other and enjoy one another's company. Ana takes great pride in caring for Mom. She is an expert negotiator and can find a way to convince Mom to do just about anything. During Mom's most belligerent and obstinate moments, Ana is truly a godsend. My mother loves to have her hair styled and, using this desire, Ana manages to convince Mom to shower, come in from the car, take her medications, eat her meals, and just about anything else she often refuses to do for others. Now that she is confined to her bed, these refusals to cooperate have stopped.

Ana drives with her sister, Celia, four hours each way twice a month from Houston to manage a five-day shift caring for Mom. Ana has not missed a shift in the ten years she has been in service to my mother. Even when Hurricane Ike demolished her home in 2008, Ana and her sister made their bimonthly pilgrimage to Dallas. Ana and her sister Celia enjoy preparing authentic Salvadorian cuisine, filling Mom's life with emotional and dietary nourishment at once. When Ana and her sister are on duty, it is as if one is stepping into the movie, *Like Water for Chocolate*. Their love for Mom is expressed in their home cooking, home remedies, singing and dancing, and in the heartfelt ways in which they care for Mom and her home.

Janie has been involved in my life at different times. She has always been an interesting person who fascinates me with her strong, take charge way of life. I first met her in the '70s when she came to work as a bartender and waitress at my restaurant.

Janie always managed the bar herself, even when serving to a full house. I was intrigued and impressed with her quick and efficient work style. Several nights after closing, she and I sat at a table drinking wine and going over the evening's funny stories and interesting characters. On those evenings, Janie shared with me the many wild times of her own life.

Prior to coming to the restaurant, Janie worked as a truck driver. I listened to story after story of how she maneuvered her truck over mountains and snowstorms, through rough terrain and bad weather, as well as late night mishaps at truck stops. Cavalier in her retelling of these incredible adventures, she fascinated and entertained me. While at the restaurant, I thoroughly respected her work ethic, initiative, unusual toughness, and joy all of which she implements in caring with my mother.

Janie is an animal lover who rescues dogs … seemingly every lost dog in the city. Her rescue mission goes far beyond simply picking up dogs she comes across in her comings and goings around town. She goes out of her way to search for dogs that are stray and in need of care. Little did I know how much Janie's "serving up" drinks, steering trucks, telling stories, and caring for strays would serve my mother who can be much like a truck and a stray herself.

When my mother initially came to live in Dallas, I naively assumed I would be her only caregiver. I quickly realized that living at my mother's house, and caring for her round the clock was an impossible task. I quickly began looking for an alternative. I had previously hired Janie to mow our lawn. One day while sitting at Mom's house contemplating the situation, I looked out the window and saw her performing her job of cutting the grass ... *Serendipity*! Having known Janie for so many years, and having witnessed her efficiency and loyalty, I knew she would be a great fit for Mom.

Janie's first night with Mom has gone down in our family history as one of the more hilarious days in my mother's many years with dementia. Janie had settled into bed in Mom's room and had the lamp on in order to do some nighttime reading. Mom, being confused as to why this strange woman was in her room, told Janie it was time for her to leave. My mother had a well perfected voice of authority from her many years as a schoolteacher, and she once again commanded Janie to leave her house that very moment. Janie, the woman who could maneuver an 18-wheeler down an icy mountain, was terrified. She called me and said, "Boss," — she has always called me Boss — "She wants me outta here." I told her to ignore Mom and convinced her to stay. Janie was extremely uncomfortable as Mom continued to shoot her the evil eye from across the room. Eventually Mom made one last attempt to rid herself of this stranger in her bedroom. She approached Janie's bed, and with all the authority and strength she could muster, she yanked the bed linens, quilt, and sheets off the bed and demanded that Janie leave the house immediately. Eventually Janie was able to distract Mom and calm her down so both could get some rest. Being the loyal person I knew Janie to be, she of course has never left my mother's employment. As a matter of fact, she rarely leaves the room without telling Mom, "I love you baby!"

When Janie first began working for my mother, I found myself in the position of protecting Mom's home from becoming a refuge for stray animals. I lectured her time and again about picking up stray dogs. I argued that she could not hold herself accountable for every dog in Dallas county. One day, after delivering one of my then infamous lectures about stray dogs, I went to the post office and fell head over heels in love with a stray puppy I found wandering the parking lot. With my own tail between my legs, I humbly brought the dog to my mother's house and permanently retired my lecture.

Virginia Vasquez was a gift from heaven sent to both my mother and me. She brought joy into Mom's home and seemed to have an innate ability to cultivate good feeling in the most bleak of moments. Virginia had a calming effect on my mother and me and brought happiness, fun, and creativity into our lives. Virginia came through a referral of a friend. At the age of fifty-two, she had several grown children, grandchildren, and one great-grandchild and was a natural caregiver. Like the others, Virginia had a special talent for lovingly manipulating my mother into doing the necessary activities Mom often refused to do.

From time to time, Virginia traveled with me out to the ranch. She was gifted in many creative pursuits: painting, drawing, and sewing. She eventually began working on mosaic pottery with me. Together we spent time on our art projects and enjoyed a reprieve from the stress of daily life. We both enjoyed tea, and during one of our afternoon conversations, we came up with a fun idea for a tea cozy business in a nearby town. We enjoyed talking about the fun we would have once Mom passed and we both had more time to dedicate to the business. Virginia had expressed a desire to be with my mother when she died, and I thought she would bring a special quality to the experience. Later I was to see the irony in this idea as events took a strange turn.

> *Develop a sense of humor about repeating yourself, as you will do it over and over and over and over and over again, one more time ...*

Bobbie is an African-American woman, and Mom took an immediate liking to her. One of Mom's dearest friends, if not her best friend, was our housekeeper Suzy who was also African-America.

Suzy worked for the family throughout my childhood and early adult life. She and Mom were always in their own world when they were together. They worked side by side completing household chores and sharing all of their life stories. They laughed together, cried together, and shared silence together in that unique way in which intimate friends relate.

Bobbie came into Mom's life long after Suzy had moved to California where she eventually died, and several years after Mom lost her ability to speak. Mom gazes for hours at Bobbie with the most adoring expression on her face, and Bobbie relishes Mom's laughter and happy spirit. I do not know if my mother confuses Bobbie with Suzy, or if Bobbie's presence simply reminds her of Suzy, but there is a genuinely special bond between the two.

We hired another caregiver, Barbara, from the same service as Bobbie to work night shifts. Barbara is sweet, quiet, and capable — the perfect night guardian.

Each of Mom's caregivers believes they are the very best. Each believes no one can care for Mom better than she. There have been countless arguments as each woman has attempted to best the other in her caregiving efforts. Their competitive caregiving brings out the referee in me; but I love every minute of it. Four women whom I love and cherish are striving to be the best at caring for the one woman I want to be cared for better than anyone in the world.

These women fill Mom's life with love and care twenty-four hours a day, seven days a week and not one has ever missed a shift, or even been late. They have become a lifeline for both Mom and me.

I know my mother is aware of the spiritual space we have created within her home. In addition, as her other abilities continue to diminish, her emotional capacities seem to flourish. She is increasingly more sensitive to the energy of others and looks deeply into the eyes of anyone she is with as though she can communicate directly with the soul. This can be rather unnerving. While she has always had good hearing, as her dementia has progressed, Mom also seems to have developed a heightened sense of hearing and responds to every small noise.

The longer her illness has endured, the more I have told her that it is okay if she wants to leave. We support her in her dying process. The last time I said this to her, tears began streaming down her cheeks.

I had thought she was deliberately holding onto life for me. I thought perhaps she was worried about me, concerned that I would not hold up if she left. I realized in that moment that she is still with us because she wants to be. Mom is holding court in her temple, and her life is fulfilling for her. Mom knows the impact her life has on us all. She knows this beautiful community is serving a greater purpose. I have promised my mother that as long as she wants to stay, we will continue to welcome the gift of her presence and relish the existence of our community.

> *Hold onto the end result of what you are trying to accomplish and let go of the attachment to how you will get it accomplished.*

Virginia Parker

The more reverence given to the process of dementia, the more it gives back.

When Kathryn's illness progressed to the point that she could no longer live independently, my sister and I converged on the house in Houston. We spent days sorting through the clutter, which had eventually evolved into a bizarre collage of important memorabilia, piles and piles of randomly placed papers, objects of varying degrees of importance, and garbage. We filled several dumpsters before editing my mother's belongings down to what could be called a normal resemblance of a lifetime's collection. We continued to live under the assumption that this "would not last long."

With money from our father's estate, we purchased the house across the street from Charlotte's home in Dallas. We hired round the clock care, and we settled into what we thought would be a short-term solution. Surrounded by all her cherished belongings, her pets, and people who care for her at every moment of the day, my mother continues to thrive. While her mind continues deteriorating, Mom's spirit and joyful presence soars.

Perhaps in hindsight, there would have been a better system of care. We never imagined the desire for life that apparently exists in every cell of Mom's body. She has always lived a lonely existence, but in her new home in Dallas she enjoys more human contact than she has ever experienced, and it is all focused directly on her. Prior to my mother's illness, I do not think I would have thought it possible to parse out one's dying in gradations as fine as she is gracefully managing to do. In preparing for what we thought were her final days, we created an atmosphere so full of love and caring attention that Mom simply refuses to part ways with this beautiful life that is so deliberately focused on her.

I have remained in Colorado and Montana and continue to make monthly visits to Dallas. Initially, I thought I was coming to visit Mom, but in reality I am coming for Charlotte. If traveling weekly to Houston was a challenge for my sister, running a full-time dementia clinic across the street while operating a restaurant still in its prime thirty years after opening its doors and playing landlord to several rental properties is itself a form of insanity. I have always been Mom's friend, but Charlotte plays the role of mother in my life. In bringing Mom home to Dallas, we inadvertently created a space that nurtures each and every one of us in ways we would never have imagined. Mom continues to flourish spiritually. Charlotte has found the mother she spent her life searching for, and I am able to give back to my sister in a way that has become a source of tremendous joy in my life.

Chapter Eight

🌳

Spiritual Dimensions of Dementia

Charlotte Parker

*Don't try to know the future. Dementia
takes its own time and goes its own way.*

As Mom continues to move deeper into
her dementia, she simultaneously
moves deeper into spiritual dimensions.
She often seems to leave us for periods of
time — periods in which she appears to be
experiencing her own world that seems to be
quite blissful. At other times, there appear
to be other entities that enter the room and
take her attention. When we speak of her
brother, mother, husband, or other people
she loved who have passed, her attention is
often drawn to other areas of the room. Her
facial expressions and dialogue suggest we
are not alone. Many times, when Mom could

still speak, she would say to me, "Where did your daddy go?" To which I would reply, "Mom, Happy has been dead for years." Inevitably she would sigh, "Well, he was right there," indicating a chair near her. At another time of my life, I would have found this to be incredibly frightening, but it is not just my mother's essence that shifts during these times. We all feel something different. It is only Mom who appears to literally see something ... well, Mom and her caregiver Virginia Vasquez.

Virginia was one of three caregivers who had cared for Mom since her dementia became severe enough to require round the clock care. When my mother reached the point in her dementia in which she could no longer manage the toilet on her own, and then eventually went to wearing diapers, she felt humiliated. Mom apologized profusely each time she had to be cleaned. Virginia was especially good in this circumstance, consoling my mother by telling her that this was her job, and she was more than happy to take care of her. Virginia acknowledged Mom's feelings while minimizing the impact of the situation. Mom learned to get through those moments with as much dignity and grace as possible.

Virginia and I had much in common, and we talked a lot about the challenges and gratifications in caring for Mom. At the same time, we often found ourselves discussing my mother's death and what that would be like. Mom's passing is a day that I both look forward to and dread, knowing I will experience both relief and grief simultaneously. Virginia was always more spiritually oriented than I. She was keenly aware of the spiritual life my mother is experiencing, and she could feel the presence of Happy, or Sonny — the name we called Mom's brother — and other entities that occasionally visit Mom.

One year, very late in my mother's dementia, many years into her bedridden phase, Happy, Mom's beloved cat named after my father, died unexpectedly. One day he was healthy and robust, and the next day he literally dropped dead, a symbolic indication of future events, as we were to understand later. Because we all — the caregivers and myself — had been expecting Mom to die "any day" for the past several years, we were all especially affected by the cat's sudden passing.

Shortly after his dying, Virginia Vasquez woke in the middle of the night to the sound of a cat scratching in the litter box. She sat up, expecting to see the second house cat, Alfred, come walking out of the bathroom, but Alfred was snuggled up against her. Both Alfred and Virginia looked curiously in the direction of the litter box only to see the spirit of Mom's dead cat, Happy, as he walked out of the bathroom and down the hall. Happy did not leave concrete evidence of his visit in the cat box, but Virginia and I did discuss the significance of this event, especially since we both thought that perhaps Happy was waiting on the other side for Mom.

Virginia always said she wanted to be with Mom at the time of her death, and I wanted her there as well. Virginia's role in our lives had taken on the form of friend, family, and spiritual guide. I knew that in Mom's final moments Virginia would know what to do.

One night while Virginia was on duty, she caught a glimpse of what she thought was an angel walking out of Mom's room — the living room — and down the hallway. Virginia described the form as very large, with a long robe and feathered wings. She believed the angel was coming for my mother. We waited. Days continued to pass.

Mom remained happy, content, and healthy. Nothing seemed out of the ordinary.

About two weeks went by and the anticipation that something of significance was about to happen eventually passed. We all remained in our normal routines. One afternoon I walked across the street looking forward to a normal afternoon of chatting with Virginia and Mom. Mom's house was designed in such a way that one entered through the living room before going into the kitchen. Once Mom became bedridden, she was stationed in the living room with a futon nearby for the caregivers to sleep on. I walked into the living room and said hello to Mom. She was happy to see me but seemed to be a little different. Her usual joyful composure was missing. Mom had not been able to speak for several years having suffered a stroke that left her without the use of language, but she had very demonstrative ways of communicating. I called for Virginia, but she did not answer. Finding that odd I continued into the kitchen. There she was — sitting on the kitchen floor, leaning against the cabinets, and not breathing.

I knew immediately that she was dead, but I was in disbelief all the same. I dialed 911 and obeyed the dispatcher as she instructed me to begin CPR. I continued CPR for the next ten minutes until the paramedics arrived and pronounced her dead. Virginia had recently been to the doctor and was given a clean bill of health. Nonetheless, she died suddenly of natural causes.

The police arrived and while they were milling about conducting their investigation, I went into the living room to be with Mom. I could tell she was aware of what had happened because, while she did not usually look worried, at this moment she looked very concerned. I will never know how long Mom had been lying in bed while Virginia sat dead on the kitchen floor, or what she might have been feeling. For myself, I was devastated and visibly shaken. I looked over at Mom and with perfect clarity she asked, "Are you all right?" Although I wasn't, I nodded yes. Just as suddenly as she spoke, she slipped back into her nonverbal mode of communicating.

I believe Virginia did see the angel in the hallway, but I now believe the angel was coming for her. I lost a dear friend. Mom lost a constant companion. As I stood devastated at her funeral, the only relief I could find was the comfort in knowing Virginia would be waiting for Mom when Mom did finally decided to make her own journey to the other side.

🌳

> *Let the person know what you are going to do before doing it; what you are doing while doing it; and what you will do next. This helps the person to feel safe and secure.*

Mom suffered a stroke several years after moving to Dallas that left her bedridden. Her doctors concluded the stroke took place in the left hemisphere of her brain due to the fact that the right side of her body was paralyzed as a result of the stroke. Interestingly, it is the right side of the brain where attributes of one's personality that are often considered to be more spiritual "reside." When a person lives mostly, or in my mother's case exclusively, in the right hemisphere of her mind, the perception of reality shifts to a more esoteric and joyful perspective.

In her book, *My Stroke of Insight*, Jill Bolte Taylor, Ph.D., a Harvard trained brain scientist who suffered a stroke in the left hemisphere of her brain and fully recovered, describes the experience of living in the right brain as nirvana. In her book she writes, "As the language centers in my left hemisphere grew increasingly silent and I became detached from my memories of my life, I was comforted by an expanding sense of grace. In this void of higher cognition and details pertaining to my normal life, my consciousness soared into an all-knowingness, a 'being at *one* with the universe' ..." This is the reality in which my mother lives and in which we choose to meet her.

The beauty of living in our "right mind" is that we do not have to suffer a stroke to shut off the left brain and move into this serene and imaginatively spiritual space. Those who practice meditation experience this reality frequently. My stepson Scott is one such person. He lives very much in his right mind. He meditates daily and understands the flow of "being one with the universe" that Dr. Taylor describes. Mom and Scott enjoy sitting together for hours communicating together on a much higher plane than those of us who are not accustomed to meditation. There is a serenity and peace in their togetherness that is palpable to everyone blessed to be present to their intimate space. Because of his spiritual practice, Scott is a unique and special companion for Mom. Together they exist in a place without time or rules.

In the right mind, the soul is able to experience pure joy without interruption from the ego that lays claim to the left brain. Ironically, in my mother's deranged state, she permanently resides in her "right" mind.

Virginia Parker

Notice the gifts.

Kathryn's journey into the depths of dementia changed all our lives in so many ways. The shrinkage of our family unit from the death of our father and grandparents was gradually reversed as our relationships with Mom's caregivers grew. Charlotte and I spend more time together than we have since childhood. While I have always considered Charlotte my mentor, we did not share common interests as children. We have now discovered many ways to connect with each other—equestrian activities, various crafts, music, bird watching, train spotting—during my trips to Texas. Mom's illness has provided an environment that nurtures our lifelong bond.

Ana, Janie, Virginia, Bobbie, Barbara, and Celia would not have entered my life were it not for Mom's illness. Their shared traits have been blessings to witness: great sense of humor and the gift of its timing as a dementia management tool; unswerving patience during frustrating experiences; complete devotion to Mom's well-being; gentleness and thorough attention to detail in caregiving functions; constancy of friendship to our family—all of them like priestesses in a temple.

Chapter Nine

The Initiation

The Greeks referred to the underworld as Eleusis—the place of happy arrival. Eventually Eleusis, or rather the initiation to the mysteries of Eleusis, came to be associated with the goal of human life. In their book, *Eleusis: Archetypal Image of Mother and Daughter*, authors Carl Kerenyi and Ralph Manheim write, "According to the sacred history of Eleusis, the first to 'arrive' was Demeter herself. The goddess was the first initiate and also the founder of the Mysteries. Her initiation was the finding of her daughter." This ancient, Greek myth illustrates the tremendous, and universal capacity all women have to love and nurture, not only their own family, but also their extended family, and community. Demeter demonstrates that there are natural seasons to life and that with sorrow also comes joy.

Eleusis is the place of happy arrival, and Demeter leads the way. Our mother was the first initiate of our family to arrive upon this place of happy arrival, and she showed us the way.

Charlotte Parker

Personal growth is inevitable throughout the dementia process.

Our mother's journey into the depths of dementia transformed our family. We changed as a familial unit, but we also changed individually, family and caregivers alike. We all found a common purpose in our lives through her, and we discovered aspects of ourselves, which until Mom's dementia, were not yet fully developed.

Our initiations were not mutually exclusive, but rather impacted each of us. In caring for my mother, my husband found a vessel for his compassion, kindness, and humor.

My initiation was the finding of my own motherhood. My mother gave me the gift of experiencing the deep and unwavering love a mother feels for her child. It was only when my mother reached the stage of her illness in which she was unable to walk, talk, or feed herself, that for the first time I could see her affection and feel her as truly present through the light in her eyes. In return, I learned to love selflessly, with no need for reciprocity. My newfound motherhood also taught me patience, and a willingness to slow down and be more present to my relationships and to my life as a whole.

Virginia Parker

Notice more gifts.

Kathryn brought a community of women together that functioned as an extended family for both Charlotte and me, as well as for one another. There is always creative energy. Whether it is Ana's and her sister's cooking, Charlotte and I enjoying a beading or art project, or Janie's creative and loving ideas for entertaining Kathryn, our mother generates a buzz of joy around her. I look forward to my trips to Dallas. Kathryn's illness draws us all together and gives us a purpose to be together.

Kathryn was never a maternal woman, and her dementia did not change her in that way for me. While I never thought of her as particularly motherly, I was not cognizant of missing the "mother experience." My initiation to Eleusis has been finding the mother I did not realize was missing — Charlotte. As Charlotte grew into her "motherhood," I found myself readily accepting the role of being mothered. I enjoy the love and attention she generously bestows upon me.

As a child, Charlotte knew what she was missing in our mother, but I did not. Charlotte's initiation into motherhood, initiated me as well. My initiation was in finding the mother I never knew was missing.

Chapter Ten

Strategies for Daily Caregiving

Charlotte Parker

Keep it simple.

One of the most important lessons I learned after many trials is really a very simple guideline: Don't argue or dispute what the demented person is claiming to be true. I now understand that Mom's reality is as real to her as my own reality is to me. Not only is it unproductive to argue with Mom, it is almost cruel in a sense. Denying my mother the validity of her experience is a discounting of her emotional expression, but the most important lesson is — *you won't win the argument anyway!*

Nor will you win the argument regarding the necessity of certain lifelong habits. Like most women, my mother took her handbag with her everywhere all the time. As she progressed in her dementia, she reached a point in which she could no longer drive, write a check, or apply her own lipstick. She came to the point of not being able to utilize any of the objects she had in her handbag, and yet she insisted on taking it with her wherever we went. If she considered it an "outing," the handbag had to come along. Even when Mom experienced Sundowner's Syndrome, she insisted on taking her handbag with her on our daily trip around the house.

At first I argued with her, trying desperately (for my own sanity) to avoid the hunt through the house for the infamously misplaced handbag. I finally had to realize a simple concept—Mom was not going anywhere without her handbag. Would I go anywhere without my handbag? As soon as I accepted that searching for the handbag and bringing it along with us was a simple part of the ritual, our outings had one less challenge to overcome.

The point is to step into the demented person's mind and embrace the world she is experiencing. By learning to be sensitive to this private realm, "the crack between two worlds," we all had an easier time adjusting to our new life.

There were times when Mom insisted on something that simply was not appropriate or interfered with a task that had to be accomplished. For example, her caregivers and I spent countless hours arguing with her, begging her, and attempting to persuade her to prepare for an outing such as a doctor appointment. Mom's response was to refuse to shower or get dressed. We then learned the value in bargaining.

Ana was a master negotiator. She knew what buttons to push with Mom to get her in action, and we took full advantage of this technique. There is no shame in bargaining. Develop a negotiating strategy and implement it. However, shaming the demented person has no place in the strategy for many reasons, but primarily because it will not work. Dementia liberates the person from societal pressures in many ways, the most basic of which is that the demented person does not care what people may think of her.

Dementia eats away at a person's independence like a hungry parasite. There will come a day in the life of every person suffering from dementia in which she is incapable of even the smallest expression of independence. Refrain from rushing that day by allowing the person as much independence as possible.

There were so many times I felt a rush of impatience and thought, *Oh just let me do that for you!* as I waited like the mother of a toddler for Mom to dress herself or complete a similar "simple" task. Finally, I was able to hold onto my awareness that Mom needed her independence even if her independence cost me "precious" time. In yielding to Mom's need for independence, I began to live each day more present to the moment. I was able to give into the "now" and fully experience my mother's reality. In the slowness of life, I experienced very sweet moments with her, as well as humorous and humbling moments. Yielding to her need for independence became yet another gift she gave me.

Practical guidelines should be established as soon as the dementia is recognized. During the time that Mom was still living independently and I made my weekly pilgrimage to Houston, I would spend hours searching for the mail. My mother had lost all ability to recognize important mail from junk mail, or real checks from bogus promotional checks. In her mind, all mail was created equal, but she had no one place for all this mail to be stored. Every Thursday I searched through the house collecting mail, discarding the junk, and securing the important documents. I do not know why it took me so long to realize the simple thing to do—have the mail forwarded to my own address.

People with dementia often become confused with where they are and why they are there and will wander away from the house. It is important to protect the home from unescorted outings. If your parent is still functioning well enough to make outings on her own, go ahead and install a deadbolt on the door that requires a key to unlock. The day will come when your parent will need to be safely secured within the home. Remove any keys that may be stored in the foyer and place them in a secure place. Keep your parent safer by implementing the following guidelines:

- Always have your parent wear an ID bracelet. You may even want to print her name and phone number inside her clothing with a permanent marker.

- Enroll your parent in the Alzheimer's Association's "Safe Return" program (even if the dementia is not Alzheimer's related).

- Install door chimes that will alert you or the caregivers when exterior doors are opened.

- Inform neighbors of your parent's condition and ask them to call you and/or the police if they see your parent out alone.

- If your parent insists on leaving the house, go with her. Do not argue or raise your voice but rather implement distractions to encourage her to return home with you as soon as possible. There is most likely a reason for her desire to leave. Step into her reality and utilize rationalizations that make sense to her.

Baby-proof the home. Similar to the developing mind of a growing baby, the deteriorating adult mind finds new and interesting discoveries with household objects that can prove quite dangerous. Take a walk through your house and pretend you do not understand the intended function of any of the items. Anything that could bring harm to a curious but naïve person should be removed and relocated to a secure place.

Prevent your parent from locking herself in the bathroom or other rooms by either replacing the interior doorknobs with lockless knobs or by placing small strips of duct tape in a crisscross pattern over the door locks. Deactivate the garage door opener so that it must be manually activated each time you go in or out. Keep the garage door clicker in a secure place. You may also want to consider placing locks on each of the home's windows. While this may seem as though you are imprisoning your parent, caring for an individual with dementia means safety is the most important priority. However, do not lock someone in the home alone. Once your parent reaches the stage of requiring this measure, she should never be left unattended. If the dementia has progressed enough that the person is not safe to be outside alone, she is also not safe inside alone.

All cabinets in the home should be perused for safety. Go through every cabinet and pantry and either discard dangerous items or place a lock on the cabinet. Cleaning supplies, gardening supplies, automotive cleaners, medications, etcetera should all be confiscated and placed in a secure location. I remember visiting my Mom and finding a bottle of bleach sitting next to a gallon of milk on the counter. That was a frightening moment.

Walk through the home and assess the wires and cords throughout the rooms. Secure everything so that the risk of your parent tripping or electrocuting herself is eliminated. This may require some creativity on your part.

Make living spaces safe by simplifying. When Mom still lived independently, I was tasked with the seemingly overwhelming chore of reducing clutter in her home. I was never able to eliminate "all the stuff," but simply managing it and editing all the clutter made her safer.

Safety Guidelines for Living Spaces

- Install smoke alarms.

- Install nightlights.

- Display stickers on each exterior window alerting emergency rescue workers of the number of residents and animals in the home.

- Display emergency numbers and the home address near all phones.

- Install an answering machine or voicemail.

- Reduce tripping hazards by moving electrical and phone cords out of the way. (You may need to actually duct tape them to the floors and walls.)

- Place colored tape on the edges of steps.

Safety Guidelines for the Bathroom

- Keep hairdryers, razors, and curling irons in a secure area.

- Remove poisons, such as drain cleaner and nail polish remover.

- Keep medications in a secure area (not in the medicine cabinet).

- Remove inside door locks so the person does not get locked inside the bathroom.

Dementia steals a person's capabilities at a rapid rate. What the person may be able to do one day, she simply cannot do the next. While your parent is still living independently be sure groceries on-hand require little to no preparation. When possible prepare food in advance. Eliminate as much day-to-day decision making necessary for your parent as possible. Reduce the number of clothes in the closet to three to five outfits that are already assembled. The same holds true for nightwear. Two to three sets of pajamas are all that is necessary — any more than that can become confusing. Discard everything else that is no longer needed.

Safety Guidelines for Other Areas of the Home

- Lock hazardous substances, such as bleach, pesticides, and paint thinners in a secure place.

- Keep the pool or hot tub areas closed or gated off.

- Set the hot water heater below 120°F.

- Keep a spare key outside the house in case your parent locks you or other caregivers out and remove inside locks such as chain locks that cannot be opened from the outside.

Reduce the kitchen supplies to only what is needed for simple meal preparation. Eliminate the items in the kitchen your parent either cannot, or should not, be using. Clean the refrigerator and pantry out a minimum of once a week. Know that your parent will not do this, and may even go behind your back and retrieve discarded items from the garbage. If possible purge the refrigerator and pantry on trash pick-up days or consider taking the garbage with you and disposing of it off-sight. This small hassle is far less trouble than continuously throwing away the same item over and over again.

Safety Guidelines for the Kitchen

- Unplug toasters and other appliances.

- Limit access to alcoholic beverages as alcohol can aggravate dementia symptoms.

- Remove or cover knobs on stoves and other appliances.

- Check food for spoilage.

Safety and organization go hand-in-hand. Do whatever is necessary including employing a housekeeper to maintain a clean and well organized environment and continuously look for opportunities to simplify your parent's life.

Virginia Parker

Get out of your own head.

I am a linear, logical, analytical person. These are not personality traits that fast-track a person to deal with dementia. I did not play with dolls as a child, did not have children, and had limited role-playing skills. Learning to deal with Kathryn's version of reality was foreign to everything I knew. Fortunately, Charlotte was eventually able to train me to give up trying to interact with our mother using our old paradigms. I will always regret that I was not as patient and kind with her in the early stages as I later learned to be.

When our mother was in her most anxious days, I tried to lecture her out of her confusion rather than understand her feelings and provide comfort. While there are obvious similarities between infancy and advanced dementia, the infant has a teachable prognosis while the dementia patient does not. Charlotte taught me to enter Mom's reality rather than try to teach her what was erroneous about it.

Chapter Eleven

Tips & Tidbits

Charlotte Parker

Always be open to tips.

Dementia is a narcissistic condition. The further Mom slipped into dementia the more she became the center of the universe — at least from her own perspective and in her own home. When I moved my mother into her home in Dallas, my intent was to create a world that was entirely focused on Mom's reality. We created a self-contained world to accommodate her every need where she did not need to worry about whether she was doing the right thing.

Mom had always been an avid shopper. Long before she moved to Dallas she had lost the ability to shop, but she still had the love of beautiful things and the desire to purchase them. Virginia Vasquez often asked Mom if she wanted to go shopping. If Mom indicated that she did, then Virginia would go through an elaborate and playful production of getting Mom dressed for the mall. She would bathe her, dress her, style her hair, and apply her make-up. Mom then grabbed her purse, and Virginia fetched a shopping basket. Mom and Virginia would then go to the "store" which consisted of the different rooms of the house no longer accessible to Mom's memory. Together they browsed the house selecting items that Mom had owned for years but had forgotten. Mom had great fun on these shopping trips. After purchasing their items, Virginia would take Mom "home" to the living room, and they selected the perfect place to display Mom's new items.

Birthdays are also fun, as the caregivers love to throw parties. They bake lovely cakes and provide ice cream, party hats, and decorations. My sister and I enjoy looking through Mom's jewelry and wrapping something we know Mom once loved. We play Mom's favorite albums, and she still thinks the musicians are in the house with us. She loves the whole scene, and we love her enthusiasm and enjoyment. Her happiness is contagious, and we all soak it up.

My sister and I used to enjoy asking Mom questions and listening to the intricate stories she told when she could speak coherently. I will never know how much of the stories she told she actually believed and how much of it was a joke she played on us. We played along with whatever she told us. Who knows, perhaps the joke was on us all along, but one thing I do know to be true — we all enjoyed it. Once when Mom was well into her dementia but still living independently, she, Virginia, and I all took a road trip to Santa Fe together and for some reason we began to talk about yodeling. Virginia asked Mom if she knew how to yodel and Mom said, "Yes, of course I do," and in total deadpan she began to sing, "woo woo woo woo." She believed that she was yodeling and that Virginia and I were ridiculous for doubting her.

Mom and Happy made smart financial investments, which afforded my mother a comfortable lifestyle. We have been fortunate that money has never been a legitimate concern for her. However, before the dementia progressed to a point that she had no understanding of money at all, she became insecure about it. She began to worry that she did not have enough. Each time we wrote a check at the grocery store Mom would comment, "Oh, I hope there is enough money in the bank to cover all this." At that point, I had not yet developed my sense of humor about the situation, and I would cringe with embarrassment. During one of my weekly visits, I took Mom's two cats to the veterinary office for their annual checkup. When I went to pay, I was charged only fifty percent of the total charges. I let the woman know that there must be a mistake and explained the bill was significantly reduced. She kindly replied that because Mrs. Parker was so poor they always gave her a fifty percent discount. I explained that was not the case at all, thanked them for their kindness and generosity, and paid the full balance. Although I was quite embarrassed, I did have a laugh in the car imagining the bizarre stories my mother must be telling all over town.

The first several years of my mother's residence in Dallas we were fortunate to have her three main caregivers appear on their own seeking employment with little effort on our part. When Virginia died, we did have to use an agency to find a replacement, and I found it very challenging to hire someone to fill the void.

When searching for an agency to provide in-home care, be sure to specify that the caregiver will need to have the necessary skills required to manage symptoms of dementia. Potential hires should be carefully screened. Include the dementia patient in the interviewing process (even if she is bedridden) so as to be able to monitor how the caregiver relates to your parent or loved one. The following questions and suggestions should provide a basic foundation for making a decision as to whether or not to move forward with a particular applicant:

- Inquire about the individual's training and certifications. Be sure to get documentation of certifications.

- Inquire about the caregiver's backup plan should he or she need to miss a scheduled shift.

- Have a candid conversation regarding the in-home chores that will be expected and make sure the person is willing to comply. Be clear that these duties may change as the dementia patient's needs change over time.

- Does the caregiver have specific medical qualifications and documentation to support the qualifications?

- Is the caregiver's CPR certification current? First Aid?

- Is he or she insured and bonded?

- Is the caregiver's mode of transportation reliable?

- Will the caregiver be able to safely transport the dementia patient to the doctor and other appointments if necessary?

Follow up and confirm any additional information provided by the prospective caregiver. If possible, secure a police background check. If the dementia patient is able to communicate verbally, allow her to ask questions of the caregiver, and the caregiver to ask questions in return. Rapport between a caregiver and the person with dementia is vital for a successful and comfortable arrangement. Regardless of how well qualified a candidate may be for the position, be aware of your gut feeling about the person and honor what your instincts tell you.

When hiring a new caregiver, you may want to schedule that person to work several shifts with the other caregivers so that the caregiver and you feel equally comfortable with the arrangement. If your parent is still able to communicate verbally, you will have to remember the feedback she provides may not be an accurate reflection of the care provided. Mom loves to tell a wild story. I can only imagine the havoc that might have ensued had I chosen to believe every story about thievery and outrageous happenings. Spend as much time with the caregivers as possible to develop your own rapport and relationship.

Developing a sense of community amongst the group is very healthy for morale and will go a long way when things get tough. While providing care, comfort, nourishment, and companionship is certainly the job of the caregiver, thank you notes, special gifts, and words of encouragement and gratitude will instill a sense of loyalty and friendship between you and the caregivers that is essential for establishing and maintaining trust.

Chapter Twelve

Giving Our Best

Charlotte Parker

Accept what is and give it time.

The care of an aging parent with a long term, debilitating illness has many challenges: logistically, practically, financially, and most certainly philosophically. Many times throughout the duration of Mom's journey into the depths of dementia, I was presented with circumstances in which I had to decide what course of treatment, action, or even non-action was truly in my mother's best interest. Is prolonging the life of a severely demented woman in her best interest? What about her financial resources? Or for that matter, is prolonging the life of a permanently debilitated person the best use of natural or human resources? None of these questions have simple, easy, or straightforward answers.

The question of "To be or not to be," took on many dimensions in my mother's scenario. My husband jokes with her saying: "OK, Kathryn, it's time to quit. All packed up yet, Kathryn? Ready for the bus to come? You don't want to miss it. Have the right change for the driver? It's time to cross over, Kathryn; the boat is waiting. Well, Mom, looks like the day is about done."

For my part, I find myself putting off my life, thinking, "I'll do this or that when Mom dies." In these moments, I long to be free of her, thinking *My God this woman is never going to die!* On the other hand, I cannot imagine the sadness that will descend on D-Day. One day I asked my sister, "How much longer?" I sat up when she replied, "When you stop needing her so much." That gave me something to think about for a while.

In terms of the concrete reality in determining a course of action in Mom's best interest, I decided on the approach of looking inward as much as possible. How would I want someone to care for me in this situation, and does Mom want the same thing I would want? I often think, *Is it best to make decisions based on who my mother is now, in each present moment, or should I make decisions based on the woman my mother once was?* There are rarely any right or wrong answers to these questions. When presented with challenges regarding Mom's health, I try to step into her reality as best I can. Before making any medical decisions on my mother's behalf, I first evaluate whether or not she is experiencing pain. If she is in pain or seems to be, and the recommended treatment would alleviate that pain, then we move forward.

We never make any specific attempts to continue her life. I try to address my mother's medical and overall care from the perspective of comfort rather than a perspective of prolonging life. Once my mother was no longer able to live independently, I quit taking her for routine medical or dental check ups. The caregivers did not support this plan of action, and I cannot blame them. No one wanted Mom to die. So, while I made executive decisions regarding Mom's health, the caregivers acted to preserve her life in their own way. On one such occasion, while still in Houston at the age of seventy-nine, Mom was rushed to the hospital by one of her caregivers while I was out of town. She had a pacemaker inserted via emergency surgery. This is not a decision I would have made. However, I can now see that my thinking around this complex issue of life and death was too narrow. Although none of us were aware of it, a process was taking place that was bringing about a transformation in us all.

I also believe that, while we usually think of death as coming in its own time, at some level the dying choose when to leave this life. Had we moved Mom into an assisted living or nursing home, she would have deteriorated far more rapidly. Even though she is deranged, bedridden, unable to feed herself or talk, Mom is happy. I believe she continues to live simply because she wants to. I can say with complete honesty that her last years have been her happiest, and so I have to think that her self-motivated prolonged life has indeed been the right choice for her.

There is no doubt that my mother's quality of care has had a direct impact on the length of her life. Still, as unpleasant as it is, the question presents itself from time to time, has personal care been the best use of my mother's financial resources? I think of all the good that could come from the many dollars spent on Mom's care throughout the years. And yet, my mother's condition has provided financial support to deserving women.

Janie funds her dog rescue business through the job my mother provides. Ana is able to bring her Salvadoran relatives for visits to Houston. She also was able to rebuild her home in Houston after hurricane Ike. It has been fascinating and inspiring to know that my mother's life and resources contribute significantly to the lives of many others in both direct and indirect ways.

In addition to my mother's round the clock care provided by her caregivers, she also has a visiting doctor and nurse practitioner. Natalie, the nurse practitioner who teaches in the Mildred Wyatt and Ivor Paul Wold Center for Geriatric Care at UT Southwestern Medical Center, often brings interns and residents with her when visiting Mom as she finds her home a useful backdrop for studying how environmental stimuli impacts a patient's health. Mom loves the attention she receives from them, and she especially perks up when male doctors and students are present. I take pride in providing an educational environment that demonstrates how someone as ill as my mother can thrive when given a space carefully created to meet her unique emotional, physical, and mental needs.

I now know that my mother did her very best in parenting me. I believe she gave me all she had to give. I can now accept that even though it was not what I wanted at the time, she gave me what she had to give. Through the process of caring for Mom, I can finally accept that "all she had to give" was indeed enough. I will never know if my mother is receiving everything she needs under my care and supervision. I can only accept that I am doing my best, mistakes and all. I am giving everything I have, and because of that, caring for my mother is the greatest gift she has ever given me.

🌳

Chapter Thirteen

A Womb with a View

Charlotte Parker

Reward yourself.

The burden and blessing of caring for an aging parent usually falls primarily on the shoulders of one family member. While support from siblings or extended family may be generous, the reality is that one person will typically step up and assume the role as primary caregiver and keeper of the purse. In our family, there was never any question as to who would take care of Mom. As a business owner, my schedule was always far more flexible than my sister's schedule. I naturally stepped into the position of caring for my mother. I often wondered how the situation might have been different had my mother become ill earlier in my career when I had several on-going businesses. I do not know how my decisions regarding Mom's care would have been different, but I cannot imagine that I would have been able to be as involved in Mom's life as I have been.

While I never held any regret about the situation, I fluctuated throughout the years in my attitude towards my sister, my resentment towards the situation itself, and a general feeling of the load being far too much for me to cope with. My emotions fluctuated as my energy level and sense of personal sacrifice fluctuated. I knew my sister also experienced a sense of guilt about the situation and that was not easy for either of us. Early in the experience we had no way of conceiving of the richness of the reward that working through the complexity of the situation would bring to our family. I could not have known I was embarking on a mysterious and ancient initiation into the dying of one self and the birthing of another.

During the early years of Mom's debilitation, I began to feel overwhelmed with the magnitude of work caring for my mother had become. I remember so many times flying home from Houston deep in disappointment and despair. I felt that all of my energy was being sucked out of me. I decided that if I was going to work myself to exhaustion for my mother, I needed to work just as hard for myself.

For several years, I had been scouring the countryside looking for a location in which to build a country inn. I wanted to call it just that — The Country Inn. I imagined a beautiful country setting, far enough outside of the city to provide an escape from urban life, but close enough that city dwellers could get away for a weekend. While I never did find the perfect place for The Country Inn, I did find the perfect place for me.

A friend called one morning to tell me about a listing in the newspaper for an eighty-acre ranch about two hours away. I immediately hung up the phone and dialed the woman who owned the property. She turned out to be a tobacco chewing, gun-slinging, teller-of-tall tales named Jackie. Jackie was a tough woman who defied the sheriff and bucked the system at every opportunity. The ranch was in a tiny town appropriately named Lone Camp. Lone

Camp consisted of a small general store, a bait shop, and a volunteer fire department. I loved it.

Lone Camp Ranch faced west, and the sun set just beyond the nearby mesa. The view from the front porch was stunning. According to local legend, if you looked at just the right time in just the right location, you could see three Indian chiefs riding off into the sunset. Jackie had scheduled the showing at sunset, and the colors of the sun as it became one with the clouds and hills were very moving. I watched the sun set over the hills, and felt as though it was a living metaphor of Mom's life — an omen that this would be a refuge for me. I took one look at the ranch and told Jackie, "I'll take it!"

While the property at Lone Camp was majestic, the house was a mess. A less inspired person would have demolished it and built from the ground up. But I had a vision. I needed a place to work off the stress, sadness, frustration, and anger that resulted from the early years of Mom's dementia.

Structurally, the house resembled a Dutch farmhouse. It had an open floor plan, two levels, a sleeping porch, and a broad front porch. Soon after buying the property I began drawing out my plans for the interior and the surrounding landscape.

I was eager to embark on what I thought would be a two-month project. My plan was to use the ranch house as canvas for my artwork. I could not wait to get started on the process of losing myself in this work and creating a haven to serve as a repose from the grind my life had become.

In the years previous, I had become involved in working with mosaic pottery. I would shop for cheap ceramics at yard sales and break them up in my studio with a hammer. The breaking itself was cathartic, and I used my imagination in re-configuring the pieces on various surfaces. While I consciously set about using the interior surfaces of the house to create a new space, I unconsciously began depicting my own myth.

Each week I conducted two pilgrimages: one to care for my mother and the other to the old ranch house to care for myself. I slowly transformed the ranch house into a mythic mosaic space depicting abstract patterns which mirrored the surrounding landscape of hills and rivers, images of mythical figures, and reflections of domestic life. Having a quiet place to escape provided a form of soul making. As I changed the space, the space changed me.

I eventually took my energy outdoors. I designed a labyrinth, planted a rose garden, and created a butterfly garden. I became a bird watcher — a passion that took on a psychological purpose of its own.

The mythologist, Joseph Campbell, popularized the notion that mythology has meaning. He referred to mythology as, "A womb with a view." A womb with a view is what I had created and what had created me. Just as the story of Demeter and Persephone mediated my initiatory trials in caring for a diseased loved one as we passed through the myth together, so also the ranch became a concrete place of rebirthing for me, rooted in archetypal, natural, and artistic images.

T.S. Eliot wrote the lines, "Our only health is the disease ... to be restored, our sickness must grow worse ..." Through the depths of my mother's dementia and my attempts to contain it, we each returned to a place of wholeness in our lives. In losing our "way," we found our selves through each other. In our return, we found our beginnings.

Resources

AARP's AgeLine® Database:
www.aarp.org/research/ageline
Find books, reports, articles & more on aging and the
50+ population. AgeLine is an online, bibliographic
database produced by AARP that focuses on the subject
of aging and middle-aged and older adults, particularly
addressing the social, psychological, economic, policy,
and health care aspects of aging.

AARP's Caregiving Resources:
www.aarp.org/foundation
This site offers a free guide to support seniors and their
families with caregiving.

AgeSource & AgeStats Worldwide:
www.aarpinternational.org/database
AgeSource & AgeStats Worldwide have been created by
AARP to facilitate the international exchange of policy
and program-relevant information in aging. AgeSource
Worldwide identifies several hundred information
resources in some 25 countries which are significant either
in size or in their unique coverage of particular aging-
related issues. The resources include, among others,
clearinghouses, libraries, databases, training modules,
major reports, and Web metasites.

AIDsmeds.com
AIDSmeds.com is dedicated to providing people
living with HIV the necessary information they
need to make empowered treatment decisions. The
founder and some of the writers of this web site
are living with HIV, and we know first hand the
challenges of learning how to fight this virus. By
offering complete, but not complicated, up-to-date
info, AIDSmeds.com seeks to help those that are
both new and old to this challenge, and to remain a
powerful resource for years to come.

Alzheimer's Associations: www.Alz.org
The Alzheimer's Association is the leading voluntary health organization in Alzheimer care, support and research.

Alzheimer's Disease: Other Forms of Dementia
www.webmd.com/alzheimers/guide/alzheimers-dementia
Learn more about other forms of non-Alzheimer's dementias.

Alzheimer's Foundation of America: www.alzfdn.org
The mission of the Alzheimer's Foundation of America is "to provide optimal care and services to individuals confronting dementia, and to their caregivers and families—through member organizations dedicated to improving quality of life."

Alzheimer's Research Forum: www.alzforum.org
This extensive networking forum is constantly updated with the latest research in Alzheimer's and dementia.

American Psychological Association: Adult Development and Aging: www.apadiv20.phhp.ufl.edu
Learn about upcoming conventions and find information on APA's latest research on aging.

Eleusis: Archetypal Image of Mother and Daughter, **authors Carl Kerenyi and Ralph Manheim**
The Sanctuary of Eleusis, near Athens, was the center of a religious cult that endured for nearly two thousand years and whose initiates came from all parts of the civilized world. Looking at the tendency to 'see visions,' C. Kerenyi examines the Mysteries of Eleusis from the standpoint not only of Greek myth but also of human nature.

Fisher Center for Alzheimer's Research Foundation:
www.alzinfo.org
The Fisher Center for Alzheimer's Research Foundation is dedicated to attacking the scourge of Alzheimer's with a 3-pronged assault focused on the cause, care, and cure for Alzheimer's disease as well as supporting the public with educational programs.

HelpGuide.org
Helpguide's mission is to help people understand, prevent, and resolve life's challenges. We empower people with knowledge and hope. Our goal is to give you the information and encouragement you need to take charge of your health and well-being and make healthy choices.

Mayo Clinic:
www.mayoclinic.com
The senior medical editors are experienced Mayo Clinic clinicians and educators who have broad knowledge of many areas of medicine, occupational health, and disease management and health promotion. They work on a daily basis with Web content producers and editors to ensure that all content is accurate, clear and relevant. Specialty medical editors are leaders in their areas of health care. They work with the site's editorial staff to generate timely, relevant and accurate information and tools.

National Center for Health Services:
www.cdc.gov/nchs/hdi.htm
Welcome! Health Data Interactive presents tables with national health statistics for infants, children, adolescents, adults, and older adults. Tables can be customized by age, gender, race/ethnicity, and geographic location to explore different trends and patterns.

National Center for Health Statistics:
www.cdc.gov/nchs/pressroom/01facts/olderame.htm
The Centers for Disease Control and Prevention's (CDC) National Center for Health Statistics (NCHS) has developed a new series of reports to focus attention on some of the most important health issues facing today's generation of older Americans. Aging Trends, produced with support from the National Institute on Aging, uses data from a variety of sources to help monitor the health and well-being of the older population. The first four reports in this new series include Trends in Causes of Death Among the Elderly, Trends in Vision and Hearing Among Older Americans, The Oral Health of Older Americans, and The Changing Profile of Nursing Home Residents: 1985-1997. Each report identifies opportunities for prevention and further research, describes those most at risk, and points to areas where increased use of existing services and aids would be beneficial.

National Council on Aging:
www.ncoa.org
The National Council on Aging is a nonprofit service and advocacy organization headquartered in Washington, DC. NCOA provides a national voice for older adults and the community organizations that serve them.

National Institute on Aging:
www.nia.nih.gov/alzheimers
The Alzheimer's Disease Education and Referral (ADEAR) Center Web site will help you find current, comprehensive Alzheimer's disease (AD) information and resources from the National Institute on Aging (NIA).

Neurology Channel:
www.neurologychannel.com/dementia
Developed and monitored by board-certified physicians,

neurologychannel provides comprehensive, trustworthy information about conditions that affect the nervous system (brain, spinal cord, nerves, and muscles), such as stroke (brain attack), Alzheimer's disease, and back pain. neurologychannel is a medical information website of Healthcommunities.com, Inc.

Science of Aging Knowledge Environment (SAGE KE): www.sageke.sciencemag.org
SAGE KE provides news, reviews, commentaries, disease case studies, databases, and other resources pertaining to aging-related research.

***The Archetypes and the Collective Unconscious -* Carl Jung**
This book is a multi-volume work containing the writings of psychiatrist Carl Jung.

The Gilbert Guide: www.gilbertguide.com
Gilbert Guide is the leading senior care Web site where families can find practical solutions, expert information and the most comprehensive senior housing guide and homecare directory for aging parents and loved ones.

The Institute for Brain Aging and Dementia (IBAD) at the University of California, Irvine: www.maryanne.bio.uci.edu
The Institute for Brain Aging and Dementia (IBAD) at the University of California, Irvine is internationally recognized for its research accomplishments in disorders of the brain, particularly those that are age-related. The Institute is UCI's center for aging and dementia research, with our faculty seeking to understand the causes leading to neurological disorders such as Alzheimer's disease, frontotemporal dementia, Lewy body dementia, and Huntington's disease. We aim to identify the life-style

factors that promote wellness and "successful aging." For those suffering from age-related memory problems, our goal is to diagnose disease, identify means for effectively treating it, and provide help to families and caregivers.

The National Hospice and Palliative Care Organization (NHPCO): www.nhpco.org
The National Hospice and Palliative Care Organization (NHPCO) is the largest nonprofit membership organization representing hospice and palliative care programs and professionals in the United States. The organization is committed to improving end of life care and expanding access to hospice care with the goal of profoundly enhancing quality of life for people dying in America and their loved ones.

The Psychological Aspects of the Mother Archetype -
Carl Jung
This collection offers a range of articles and extracts from Jung's writings on marriage, Eros, the mother, the maiden, and the anima/animus concept. In the absence of any single formal statement by Jung on the psychology of women, this work conveys his views on the feminine and on topics that are intrinsic or related.

The Roy M. and Phyllis Gough Huffington Center on Aging: www.hcoa.org/newsite/index.asp
The Roy M. and Phyllis Gough Huffington Center on Aging is committed to addressing the needs of an aging population by providing medical education and training, conducting basic and clinical science research, and delivering healthcare through BCM affiliated hospitals and other institutions. Today, the Huffington Center on Aging is recognized as one of the premier aging centers in the United States and the world.

The University of North Texas Libraries:
www.library.unt.edu/media/rental-collections/fvca
The Film & Video Collection on Aging is intended to
make audio-visual media on aging available to the widest
possible audience. The Collection is home to over 700
audio-visual titles concerned with different aspects of
aging and long-term care, from feature films to clinical
programs. The UNT Media Library maintains and
circulates this collection of 16mm films and videos. The
Film & Video Collection on Aging at UNT consists of two
originally separate collections: the Gerontological Film
& Video Collection (GFVC) and the National Media Owl
Award Video Collection (Owl).